Transforming Towards
Life-Centered Economics

Transforming Towards Life-Centered Economics

How Business, Government, and Civil Society Can Build a Better World

Sandra Waddock

BEP

BUSINESS EXPERT PRESS

Leader in applied, concise business books

Transforming Towards Life-Centered Economics: How Business, Government, and Civil Society Can Build a Better World

Copyright © Business Expert Press, LLC, 2020.

Cover design credit: Sandra Waddock

Interior design by Exeter Premedia Services Private Ltd., Chennai, India

First published in 2020 by
Business Expert Press, LLC
222 East 46th Street, New York, NY 10017
www.businessexpertpress.com

ISBN-13: 978-1-95253-870-4 (paperback)
ISBN-13: 978-1-95253-871-1 (e-book)

Business Expert Press Business Ethics and Corporate Citizenship Collection

Collection ISSN: 2333-8806 (print)
Collection ISSN: 2333-8814 (electronic)

First edition: 2020

10 9 8 7 6 5 4 3 2 1

Printed in the United States of America.

Dedication

For Ben and Alan. You are the light that, as Leonard Cohen sang and wrote, the cracks let in.

For Steve Waddell and all the change makers in the SDG Transformation Forum, WEAll, and in so many other places, who are trying to bring about the better world so desperately needed.

Abstract

Transforming Towards Life orients change agents, policy makers, activists, business leaders, ecologists, economists, and thoughtful people everywhere to the values and practices needed to build a world where all can flourish, where "all" includes all humanity and all of life's beings. It provides an in-depth understanding of what it will take, especially in the wake of the global Covid-19 pandemic and the burgeoning climate emergency, to transform today's growth- and profit-oriented socioeconomic systems to life-affirming ways benefit all rather than just an elite few. *Transforming Towards Life* argues that to move towards a world in which all can flourish, we all need to start telling new, yet very ancient, stories about who we are and why we are here in the world—stories built on relationship or connectedness, responsibility for the whole, reciprocity, and equity. We need to incorporate core ideas about what gives life to systems into all businesses, communities, governments, and other types of organizations—that is, what helps them flourish. Business and other institutions need to create collective value, that is, value for all, and change the mindsets of people engaged with them so that they in turn can generate new performance metrics, practices, and power relationships that enable people everywhere to find their voice and their capacity to participate actively in bringing about a flourishing world. The book concludes with thoughts about how each one of us can do our bit to bring about this necessary transformation.

Keywords

system transformation; flourishing; life-centered economies; stories; narratives; life; values; Indigenous wisdom; sustainability; business transformation

Contents

Preface xi

Chapter 1   What Is Wrong? 1

Chapter 2   Look in the Mirror: Self-Induced Systemic Crises 19

Chapter 3   Neoliberalism and the Need for Transformation 35

Chapter 4   Stories, Narratives, and Memes:
Foundations of Cultural Mythologies 53

Chapter 5   Accomplishing Transformational System Change 71

Chapter 6   Emerging a Life-Centered Worldview 85

Chapter 7   Towards Flourishing Life and Creating
Collective Value 103

Chapter 8   Stewardship of the Whole: Beyond Sustainability
to Flourishing 123

Chapter 9   New Economies Oriented towards Life 147

Chapter 10 So What? What's Next? What Can You Do? 169

About the Author 181

Index 183

Preface

This book offers an alternative way of thinking about our—human—relationships to each other, to nature, to businesses and other institutions, and to wealth than is dominant in much of the so-called developed world. It offers a way of thinking about transforming what we today call our economies—but that really are our societies with their embedded economies. It is not necessarily a new way, though. In fact, it is based in many ways on ancient wisdom—Indigenous wisdom and principles that give life to systems—that can help each of us do our part to transform our world for the better. Through these pages, I want to tell a new and very old socioecological-economic story that can potentially help us all shape a better future together. It is a story that places humans *into* nature, as *part* of her majesty and shifts economic thinking towards collective value[1] for all.

This story is about creating a flourishing world of equity and dignity for all, where "all" includes nonhuman beings, too. It is about an emerging understanding of our interconnectedness—with each other and with nature. It is a story that recognizes that because we are interconnected and interdependent with nature humans can flourish only when nature flourishes. It is a story about working together to create and institutionalize this new story. It is a story about new—or very ancient—ways of being on the earth that provide meaningful ways for people to "be" and to connect with each other, including work that matters. New ways that draw in many respects from old ways that worked for millennia that need to be translated into today's norms and living standards.

As I write these words, the world is facing the devastating impact of the novel Coronavirus/Covid-19 in 2020. "Normal" economic and social systems have all been turned upside down; people have been told to stay and sometimes work from home; whole economies have been fundamentally

---

[1] Donaldson, T., and J.P. Walsh. 2015. "Toward a Theory of Business." *Research in Organizational Behavior* 35, pp. 181–207.

shut down, except for what are recognized as essential services. The whole experience has upended commonly held beliefs and is forcing many people to rethink how they—and we all—live in this world together.

Once the crisis passes, there will undoubtedly be significant attempts to return the world to what was once considered normal. Indeed, such efforts are already beginning. Many people in power already want our human socioeconomic systems to return to the economic ways that have been dominant since the so-called Reagan–Thatcher revolution of 1980, which put in place the economic ideology known as neoliberalism. That ideology has been sorely tested during the Covid-19 outbreak—and found wanting. It has hurt too many people and sent the earth's capacity to support human civilization off a climate change cliff.

Collectively, we have an opportunity to change that now. But transformation can only happen if many more of us recognize that this system we believe is "normal" is highly problematic. It will happen only if we can tell ourselves a new story that helps us transform the world—to "build back better" as disaster response recovery experts say, not to return to the same old, same old ways. It will happen only if we then act upon this new story to make it real—to bring its precepts into practice. It is up to us. As the cartoon character Pogo said, "We have met the enemy and it is us."

More to the point, though, as Mahatma Gandhi said and many shamans say, "Be the change you want to see in the world."

Businesses, our political institutions, and the organizations of civil society, along with each of us individually and collectively, share the responsibility for creating a more just, equitable, and flourishing future for all. Business, in particular, as perhaps the most powerful of today's institutions play a vital role in shaping a transformed future—and will need to transform themselves as part of that process. But the systems that surround businesses—the ecosystem of social pressures and constraints, expectations and demands, and policy guidelines and requirements—is also vitally important because no institution, whether business or government, can make the significant changes that are needed without the whole ecosystem shifting, too.

I hope you will join in this journey towards well-being, equity, and flourishing for all through the creation of an economy and set of institutions that enhance life rather than wealth.

Transforming Towards Life aims to provide direction to a future in which all—humans, other living creatures, our institutions—business and other—and our natural ecosystems—can flourish. Of course, no one has the "answer" because this transition is a road yet untraveled. There is no roadmap. We can perhaps all imagine a world in which all humans, other living beings, and ecosystems experience well-being and the dignity that their very existence demands. A world in which all of life flourishes. To bring about a new vision, I will argue, it first needs to be articulated as a new story or narrative, supported by resonant memes. Then people with the capability of acting, no matter where they are in the world and no matter how big or small their contribution may be, need to do their part to bring about the change, creating new metrics and new systems oriented towards an encompassing yet flexible new vision.

This approach to system transformation means fundamentally rethinking today's dominant narrative, which has led us to today's ecological and social crisis points. We need to reframe how we—humans—relate to each other, to our societies and the economies that they spawn, and, importantly, how we relate to nature. In short, we need a new narrative and a new set of supporting memes (core ideas) to support a positive relationship between humans and the world around us, particularly today with respect to businesses and economies. Only then can the mindset shift, and the ability to transcend mindsets, that Donella Meadows argued are the most powerful levers of change begin.[2] We need to find ways to enact or bring about this new narrative into the reality of day-to-day human and natural existence. That enactment involves reshaping both our major institutions like businesses and the societal contexts in which they operate so that expectations of what businesses do and why itself transforms.

A new narrative needs to inform our attitudes and beliefs and ultimately the behaviors and practices not just of individual humans and local communities, but also of all of our public or governmental institutions, businesses, and civil society institutions. In other words, we need to move beyond—transcend and include in many ways—the old narrative,

---

[2]   Meadows, D. 1999. "Leverage Points: Places to Intervene in a System." Harland, VT: The Sustainability Institute. Posted at: http://donellameadows.org/archives/leverage-points-places-to-intervene-in-a-system/

accepting and understanding its beneficial aspects, while simultaneously recognizing that it no longer serves the world we are actually living in.

Before launching into this book, I want to acknowledge the many people who have been working on transforming societies and economies for years. I have benefited here from their wisdom. Without these efforts, none of these ideas could have come to fruition. While I cannot name all of them, some key influences need to be mentioned:

- The SDG Transformations Forum and its many participants, founded by Steve Waddell, and in which I am also participating, including the Bounce Beyond team
- WEAll, the Wellbeing Economy Alliance, and its progenitors, including the emerging WEAll USA working group, and all of its allies
- The Humanistic Management Network and International Humanistic Management Association and its leaders
- My Social Issues in Management and other Academy of Management colleagues
- My colleagues at Boston College
- All of my collaborators and mentors over the years
- Too many others for my poor brain to remember.

Sandra Waddock
Newton, MA
2020

CHAPTER 1

What Is Wrong?

Today's economic system works quite well—for the already well-off, as the global Covid-19 pandemic aptly demonstrated. It works substantially less well for the vast majority of people in the United States, who were already struggling to earn a decent living prior to the pandemic and whose situation became even more evident in the wake of the novel Coronavirus, Sars-Cov-2. In the United States, for example, workers' wages were basically flat for about 40 years,[1] even before the massive unemployment caused by the pandemic. There is even an emerging group that Guy Standing calls the "precariat,"[2] comprised of "millions of people scattered around the world, living and working in insecure jobs and conditions of life."[3] This instability and uncertainty—even before the pandemic—is a consequence of today's capitalism—manifested as neoliberalism—and unrelenting pressures for globalization of business and economies.

Today's economic system and associated social supports work even less well for the billions of people globally still living in relatively abject poverty. Despite some progress made on the UN's aspirational Sustainable Development Goals (SDGs), the UN concluded in 2019 that much more need to be done to achieve these aspirations for a world of peace and prosperity for people and planet.[4] The current system is working not

[1] DeSilver, D. 2018. "For most US Workers, Real Wages have Barely Budged in Decades." *Pew Research Center FactTank*, August 7, 2018, https://pewresearch.org/fact-tank/2018/08/07/for-most-us-workers-real-wages-have-barely-budged-for-decades/ (accessed April 13, 2020).

[2] Guy Standing. 2012. "The Precariat: From Denizens to Citizens?" *Polity* 44, no. 4, pp. 588–608.

[3] Guy Standing. 2012. "The Precariat: From Denizens to Citizens?" *Polity* 44, no. 4, pp. 588–608, p. 589.

[4] United Nations. 2019. "The Sustainable Development Goals Report 2019." https://unstats.un.org/sdgs/report/2019/The-Sustainable-Development-Goals-Report-2019.pdf, (accessed April 13, 2020).

much at all for producing a sustainable natural environment for humanity or the planet's other living entities and ecosystems, as many scientific reports forcefully argue,[5] particularly since one of the SDGs (#8) calls for continual growth and "economic development," an ecologically problematic notion, which very much frames the goals in the context of today's economics.

How the world operates today is based on a story. It is a story that we humans, at least in the so-called developed world of Western thought, have told ourselves for hundreds, even thousands, of years. In that story, humans dominate and control nature. This story tells us that we humans can and should exploit nature's resources, working self-interestedly to grasp as much of her wealth for ourselves as possible. This (in my view) misguided belief about human dominance of nature fatefully combines with a more recent economic narrative of neoliberalism, which argues for the production of financial wealth above any possible other forms of wealth.

Today's dominant story, even in the face of the Covid-19 pandemic, is still neoliberalism. Neoliberalism, as we will explore in detail later, argues for individual but not shared responsibility, and for "free markets" that will magically solve all social and human problems if simply left alone. It argues for endless economic growth without regard for the social or ecological consequences of that growth. Importantly, it also argues for small governments that protect private property and individuals while ignoring social and natural well-being. The global Covid-19 pandemic, if nothing else, has put to rest these myths.

---

[5] Among many others: Diaz, S., J. Settele, and E. Brondizio. 2019. "Summary for Policymakers of the Global Assessment Report on Biodiversity and Ecosystem Services of the Intergovernmental Science-Policy Platform on Biodiversity and Ecosystem Services, IPBES." https://ipbes.net/sites/default/files/2020-02/ipbes_global_assessment_report_summary_for_policymakers_en.pdf (accessed May 3, 2020); Ripple, W.J., C. Wolf, T.M. Newsom, P. Barnard, W.R. Moomaw and 11258 others. 2019. "World Scientists' Warning of a Climate Emergency." Bioscience, https://academic.oup.com/bioscience/advance-article/doi/10.1093/biosci/biz088/5610806?searchresult=1; IPCC (Intergovernmental Panel on Climate Change), 2018. Global Warming of 1.5 C: All Chapters. 2018. http://ipcc.ch/report/sr15/ (accessed April 20, 2020).

Transforming towards Valuing Life

Economics and business practices need to be reoriented to what an economy should actually deliver: an equitable distribution of wealth, health and wellbeing, while protecting the planet's resources for future generations and other species. By reorienting goals and expectations for business, politics and society, we can build a wellbeing economy that serves people and planet. A wellbeing economy will put people at the centre of a new economic purpose and close the gulf between the economy and democratic control. It will deliver good lives for people first time around, rather than requiring so much effort to patch things up. It will not harm people and the environment, and so will avoid having to deliver expensive downstream intervention to fix the damage caused by an economic model fixed on growth.[6]

This statement represents the thinking of a coalition of people from many different institutions around the world called WEAll, the Wellbeing Economy Alliance.[7] These people and many of the groups and networks they represent are working together to build a better world, in part by telling a new story about human beings and how we live and work together with planet earth.

The still emerging story, which is actually an ancient story that draws on Indigenous wisdom and Eastern thought as well as principles that give life to systems, places us humans firmly *in* nature. It recognizes that we are dependent on and interdependent with nature's bounty, and aware of her potentialities and the limits imposed by her constraints. It is a story that can be retold in many different ways by diverse people who have vastly dissimilar agendas—and who all want a better world, a more just, equitable, and flourishing world, for their children's children.

---

[6] Wellbeing-Economy Alliance (WEAll) Brochure. 2019. https://wellbeingeconomy.org/wp-content/uploads/2019/03/WEAll-brochure_INEdits_Final2.0.pdf (accessed April 13, 2020) p. 9.

[7] For more details, see https://wellbeingeconomy.org/

These ideas arise out of a recognition that today's dominant story, embodied in the tenets of neoclassical economics (otherwise known as neoliberalism) and in the story of man's [sic] "dominion" over nature, is no longer working. The novel Coronavirus, if nothing else, demonstrated that reality in 2020, as social support, employment, and governmental system, not to mention health systems, strained and in many ways broke under its impact. While today's dominant story has been incredibly useful in pulling many people out of poverty around the world and in creating the technologically sophisticated and interconnected world familiar in the "developed" parts of the world today, it doesn't work for vast majority of people. That story is certainly not working for the many other creatures of the world, who are now undergoing what has been termed the sixth great extinction that now threatens one to two million species.[8] Possibly most importantly, this system doesn't work for the natural environment's capacity to support human civilization as we know it over the longer term.[9]

We need a new story or set of stories. We also need powerful and resonant new memes to support that story and engender new and different mindsets, practices, policies, and institutions. These new mindsets and practices need to be life-affirming for *all* living beings, other living beings, and natural ecosystems as well as for humans. They need to honor Indigenous and traditional values of relationship, responsibility, reciprocity, and redistribution to emerge an equitable, just, and flourishing world for all. They need to be based in values of dignity, well-being, and equity for all. They need to be supported by markets that go beyond "free" to become fair and provide decent and meaningful work to all capable people. They need to be supported by business models and accounting systems that

---

[8] Diaz, S., J. Settele, and E. Brondizio. 2019. "Summary for Policymakers of the Global Assessment Report on Biodiversity and Ecosystem Services of the Intergovernmental Science-Policy Platform on Biodiversity and Ecosystem Services, IPBES." https://ipbes.net/sites/default/files/2020-02/ipbes_global_assessment_report_summary_for_policymakers_en.pdf (accessed April 13, 2020).

[9] Ripple, W.J., C. Wolf, T.M. Newsom, P. Barnard, W.R. Moomaw, and 11258 others. 2019. "World Scientists' Warning of a Climate Emergency." Bioscience, https://academic.oup.com/bioscience/advance-article/doi/10.1093/biosci/biz088/5610806?searchresult=1 (accessed April 13, 2020).

take full costs of production of goods and services into consideration. They need to be articulated by economic models that redefine development and efficiency in ways that support the planet's ability to generate well-being and dignity or what for short I will call flourishing for all, without further depleting natural resources or impoverishing people and states. In fact, these new stories need to be aimed at regenerating and restoring our world to a better state than it currently is in. They need to be oriented towards goals of well-being and dignity for all, rather than profits for the few. They need to be built on metrics and measurement systems that take these broader, holistic goals into account.

The chapters that follow explore these ideas in much more detail and hopefully illustrate pathways for moving individuals, communities, societies, and businesses in these new directions. Before we get there, however, it is important to understand today's dominant story, the memes that support it, and a bit about where and why it has gone wrong.

Today's Cultural Mythologies

If you listen to or read the news, you are undoubtedly familiar with what anthropologists call cultural mythologies,[10] the stories and ideas that shape understandings of what the world is and how it works. In some ways, these stories are so embedded in most of our thinking that it is sometimes hard to recognize them as just stories—myths—that we tell ourselves about how the world works. Saying that these dominant narratives are "just stories," however, is to belie the power that they have to shape beliefs, attitudes, and, ultimately, behaviors and practices.

Today's cultural mythologies in the "developed," Western, industrialized parts of the world, first of all, are deeply embedded with thinking that derives from the period called the Enlightenment, also sometimes known as the Age of Reason, during the 18th century. Enlightenment ideas revolving around the primacy of scientific knowledge, empirical evidence, and reason over religious beliefs still pervade thinking today. When such beliefs emerged, they had the impact of decreasing peoples'

---

[10]   Dow, J. 1986. "Universal Aspects of Symbolic Healing: A Theoretical Synthesis." *American Anthropologist* 88, no. 1, pp. 56–69.

willingness to bow to authority and tradition, that is, to religious and political leaders, rules, and other authority figures who had been dominant before scientific beliefs took hold.

The Enlightenment replaced these older ways of interacting with the world with scientific understanding, data, and reason. Deeply embedded in the U.S. Constitution, Enlightenment ideas overthrew (at least in theory) the notion that men should dominate women, that authority figures of all sorts, whether church, aristocratic, or political, necessarily held both wisdom and the rightful power to enforce their dictates over people.[11] They also, however, entrenched ideas about rationality, reason, and the scientific method, with its powerful emphasis on empiricism and what has come to be known as positivism (i.e., emphasizing empirical facts), as the way the world works.

In many respects, Enlightenment ideas supported empiricism, rationality, logic, mathematical proofs, and purportedly "objective" ways of knowing to the near-exclusion of subjective insights and experiences, not to mention theology and religion or any form of metaphysics. They, along with the philosopher René Descartes, who is famous for his statement that "I think, therefore I am," were influential in Western thinking. This thinking separated mind from body rather than viewing humans as integral wholes with both subjective and objective qualities. In this positivist worldview, intuition, inspiration, reflection, and introspection, and even qualitative understandings and research, are not useful ways of learning and knowing. Enlightenment thinking argues that the social order, like the natural order, derives from general laws that can be discovered and are scientifically verifiable.

---

[11] Szalay, J. 2016. "What Was the Enlightenment?" LiveScience, July 7, 2016, http://livescience.com/55327-the-enlightenment.htmlf (accessed May 26, 2020); also Brooks, D. 2017. "The Enlightenment Project." New York Times (accessed February 28, 2017) https://nytimes.com/2017/02/28/opinion/the-enlightenment-project.html (accessed May 26, 2020); and Soll, J. 2015. "The Culture of Criticism: What Do We Owe the Enlightenment?" New Republic, May 20, 2015, https://newrepublic.com/article/121837/what-do-we-owe-enlightenment (accessed May 26, 2020).

Values associated with the Enlightenment are deeply embedded into the U.S. Constitution (and also the founding documents of some other nations, including France), including principles of reason, scientific method, and both political and individual liberty. Add to these values, the secularization of learning and separation of church and state, religious tolerance and skepticism. Further, the Enlightenment developed the idea of human, social, and technological progress, a view now deeply embedded in Western thinking, along with a foundation of empiricism or "objective truths"[12] rather than faith as a basis of knowledge. Personal experience and subjectivity were downplayed. Even the idea of human rights derives from Enlightenment thinkers.[13] What followed was a rather mechanistic conception of the world and how it works, accompanied by a view that humans are fundamentally rational moral beings who operate largely individualistically and in their own self-interest.[14]

This move towards science also devalued traditional Indigenous wisdom, which tends to be nature- and place-centric as well as highly relational with all beings, rather than human-centric.[15] Many Indigenous cultures place important value on relationships, which are nurtured through practices of reciprocity, redistribution, and taking responsibility for the whole community.[16] Approaches to the world in Indigenous cultures tend to emphasize holistic perspectives on humans' place *in* (not separate from) nature, as interdependent and connected with the whole and all of its other living beings. In that sense, humans or "man" is not

---

[12] Zakai,A. 2006. "The Age of Enlightenment." *The Cambridge Companion to Jonathan Edwards*, 80–99. Cambridge UK: Cambridge.

[13] Szalay 2016; Brooks 2017; Soll 2015.

[14] Zakai 2006.

[15] I use these ideas humbly and with recognition that I am a white woman of privilege working in a colonialized environment.

[16] Harris, L., and J. Wasilewski. 2004. "Indigeneity, An Alternative Worldview: Four R's (Relationship, Responsibility, Reciprocity, Redistribution) vs. Two P's (Power and Profit). Sharing the Journey Towards Conscious Evolution." *Systems Research and Behavioral Science: The Official Journal of the International Federation for Systems Research* 21, no. 5, pp. 489–503.

separated from nature, and responsibility is taken for the care or steward-ship of the whole.[17]

Economics as we know it today also devalues life itself. Yet princi-ples that give life to human (socioeconomic) systems, including purpose, boundedness, novelty, connectedness, diversity, and wholeness,[18] are vital to building a flourishing world. The book will come full circle back to these ideas towards the end for they form the centerpiece of possible new narratives that will influence attitudes, behaviors, and practices in our world.

Today, Enlightenment beliefs are augmented by other powerful and compelling beliefs and concepts that underpin the economic narrative, a narrative that drives the ways that businesses and economies work. This narrative, like that of the Enlightenment, suggests how we humans (should) relate to major institutions like businesses and governments, as well as to each other. Based on a largely quantitative approach to the "science" of economics, this approach makes a number of critical assump-tions about human nature and human societies. Known as neoliberalism, the narrative finds its most potent manifestation in the doctrine, even dogma, of neoclassical economics. Neoliberalism is based on a core set of beliefs, evidenced as memes or core cultural artifacts, which include words, ideas, images, phrases, symbols, and artistic expressions that shape beliefs, attitudes, and practices.[19]

These dominant economic (and business) memes include ideas about free markets, private property, free trade, laissez-faire governments, and continual "progress." Importantly, humans in this conception are

---

[17] Edwina Pio and I have discussed these ideas in a paper, Invoking Indigenous Wisdom for *Management Learning*, in press 2020.

[18] Kuenkel, P., and S. Waddock. 2019. "Stewarding Aliveness in a Troubled Earth System." *Cadmus* 4, no. 1, pp. 14–38; also, Waddock, S., and P. Kuenkel. 2019. "What Gives Life to Large System Change?" *Organization and the Natural Envi-ronment*, DOI: https://journals.sagepub.com/doi/10.1177/1086026619842482

[19] Susan Blackmore has best articulated the functioning and power of memes. Blackmore, S. 2000. *The Meme Machine*, Vol. 25. Oxford Paperbacks; Black-more, S., L.A. Dugatkin, R.B. Peter, J. Richerson, and H. Plotkin. 1997. "The Power of Memes." *Scientific American* 283, no. 4, pp. 64–73; and Susan, B. 1997. "The Power of the Meme." *Skeptic* 5, no. 2, pp. 43–49.

assumed to be free, rational, and predominantly self-interested. In that list, the links to Enlightenment values of rationality, freedom, and liberty, and even individualism are evident. Constructed into a narrative about how the economy should work, tenets of neoliberalism and neoclassical economics can be summarized as follows:

> Businesses and economies operate best with free markets, free economies, and free trade on a global scale, that is, with as few rules and restrictions as possible. Growth is a core objective of this system because free and unregulated markets are expected to benefit everyone. Further, free markets take care of most if not all problems. The bottom line is financial wealth, measured in maximized shareholder wealth and profitability for businesses and growth in gross domestic/national product for countries/societies (or, as they are known, "economies"). Private property is a core value. Thus privatization of what might have once been considered public goods is advocated. Further, "laissez-faire" government, that is, deregulation or as little government regulation/intervention in markets as possible, is favored, since such regulation might reduce profits. Competition, among businesses and even nations, is a hallmark of the free enterprise system as thus defined, with a winner-take-all attitude based on individualism and libertarianism, free trade, economic freedom, and social Darwinism, favoring policies that include economic liberalization, privatization, fiscal austerity, deregulation, free trade, and spending limitations for governmental agencies.[20]

Collectively, this narrative and its supporting memes create an "economistic" paradigm about businesses, economies, and even human beings.[21] Economistic thinking contrasts with the more humanistic paradigm with

---

[20] Waddock, S. 2016. "Foundational Memes for a New Narrative About the Role of business in society." *Humanistic Management Journal* 1, no. 1, pp. 91–105.
[21] Pirson, M. 2017. *Humanistic Management: Protecting Dignity and Promoting Well-Being.* Cambridge University Press.

which this chapter opened, and which is currently competing with the older economistic one.[22]

The dominant paradigm of neoliberalism has resulted in globalized markets, a growth-at-all-costs mentality among businesses and economies, and a great deal of wealth for the already wealthy. It has also generated growing inequality, a climate change crisis, a human-caused sixth great extinction of species,[23] massive topsoil erosion, inhumane agricultural practices, significantly divisive politics, the opportunity for uncontrolled pandemics like Covid-19, and numerous other social and ecological ills. While this system has allowed many people to emerge from abject poverty, at the same time it has left many others behind and generating potentially socially destabilizing gaps between rich and poor. All the while it creates a potentially existential set of ecological and social threats for humanity.

I will explore these ideas in more detail later. Here, let it suffice to say that several important factors contribute to problematic states for many people: the availability of meaningful and decent work, a climate and natural environment that supports the human project while not destroying the natural environment, and sufficient equity in the system to support a sense of fairness and open possibilities for all. Below, we briefly examine the issues associated with each of these important aspects of well-being, dignity, and an economy in service to life.

So What Has Gone Wrong?

The world is not in good shape ecologically, which will be discussed in more depth in the next chapter, or socioeconomically, as outlined below.

---

[22]   Laszlo, C., S. Waddock, and R. Sroufe. 2017. "Torn Between Two Paradigms: A Struggle for the Soul of Business Schools." *AI Practitioner* 19, no. 2, and Michael. P. 2017. *Humanistic Management: Protecting Dignity and Promoting Well-Being*. Cambridge University Press.
[23]   Diaz, J.S., and E. Brondizio. 2019. "Summary for Policymakers of the Global Assessment Report on Biodiversity and Ecosystem Services of the Intergovernmental Science-Policy Platform on Biodiversity and Ecosystem Services." *IPBES*. URL: https://ipbes.net/sites/default/files/2020-02/ipbes_global_assessment_report_summary_for_policymakers_en.pdf (accessed May 3, 2020).

Political divisiveness, populism, and partisanship, climate change, growing inequality, pandemic potential, various impending sustainability crises, and terrorism and many other ills send clear signals that something needs to change and change radically. Importantly, today's system, particularly our economic system, is rooted in an increasingly outdated understanding of the purposes and functioning of businesses.

The purpose of business under neoliberal thinking is frequently and deliberately articulated as maximizing wealth for one group of stakeholders—shareholders. As some legal scholars argue, however, that sense of purpose rests on a misunderstanding of the law.[24] That misunderstanding, however, is important because businesses are certainly among if not actually today's most dominant and powerful institutions. Many companies have global reach and impact on both individuals as customers, employees, and investors, and on whole nations. All of these factors (and others) lead to problems in generating flourishing for all and an economy that serves life not wealth. Below are just a few of the imbalances and significant issues that today's economic and business systems have generated.

Inequality: Wealth for the (Very) Wealthy

On the one hand, the wealthy are doing very well. In a 2017 report titled "An Economy for the 99%," Oxfam found that just eight men control as much wealth as the bottom 3.6 billion people in the world, and the richest 1 percent owned more wealth than 99 percent of the rest of humanity.[25] That report was updated in 2020 to indicate that 2,153 billionaires control more wealth than 60 percent of the world's population, with the number of billionaires having doubled since 2010.[26]

---

[24] Stout, L.A. 2012. *The Shareholder Value Myth: How Putting Shareholders First Harms Investors, Corporations, and the Public.* Berrett-Koehler Publishers.

[25] Oxfam Briefing Paper. January 16, 2017. "An Economy for the 99%." https://oxfam.app.box.com/v/an-economy-for-99-percent/1/15862322999/122574711571/1 (accessed January 20, 2020).

[26] Lawson, M., A. Parvez Butt, R. Harvey, D. Sarosi, C. Coffey, K. Plaget, and J. Thekkudan. 2020. "Time to Care. Oxfam Policy Papers." https://oxfam.org/en/research/time-care (accessed April 14, 2020).

The 2019 Oxfam report on inequality noted that men own 50 percent more of global wealth than women. Further, men control more than 86 percent of corporations, while unpaid care work is estimated at around $10 trillion (yes, that is a "t"). Oxfam estimated that the world's billionaires' wealth was increasing on an average of $2.5 billion a day by 2019.[27] The trends around equality clearly are not getting better.

One Oxfam report reached a stark conclusion: "Left unchecked, growing inequality threatens to pull our societies apart … It leaves more people living in fear and fewer in hope."[28] This position has already been acknowledged by business leaders in the World Economic Forum. In discussing global risks around inequality, these leaders suggest that there is a real potential for a dystopian global future,[29] a future that became manifest during the Covid-19 crisis in many ways and point to the stark realities and failings of today's human systems. Such economic stratification, that is, the well-off commanding ever-more of the resources and wealth to the exclusion of the masses, that is, growing inequality may be a recipe for civil unrest.[30]

The Future of Jobs

Add to inequality a growing global jobs crisis and the inequality crisis does not seem to have a good trajectory. For one thing, technological advances,

---

[27] Oxfam. 2019. "5 Shocking Facts About Extreme Global Inequality and How to Even It Up." https://oxfam.org/en/even-it/5-shocking-facts-about-extreme-global-inequality-and-how-even-it-davos, (accessed April 6, 2019).

[28] Oxfam Briefing Paper, An Economy for the 99%, p. 2.

[29] World Economic Forum, Global Risks 2012, Seventh Edition, 2012, http://reports.weforum.org/global-risks-2012/?doing_wp_cron=1478086016.053333 9977264404296875 (accessed May 26, 2020).

[30] Diamond, J. 2001. *Collapse: How Societies Choose to Fail or Succeed*. Penguin; Weiss, H., and R.S. Bradley. 2001. "What Drives Societal Collapse?" *Science* 291, no. 5504, pp. 609–10; Motesharrei, S., J. Rivas, and E. Kalnay. 2014. "Human and Nature Dynamics (HANDY): Modeling Inequality and Use of Resources in the Collapse or Sustainability of Societies." *Ecological Economics* 101, pp. 90–102; and Ahmed, N. 2014. "Nasa-Funded Study: Industrial Civilisation Headed for 'Irreversible Collapse'?" *The Guardian* 14, no. 14, 337–36, http://elegantbrain.com/edu4/classes/readings/depository/class/inequality_civiliz_collapse.pdf (accessed May 26, 2020).

artificial intelligence, and digitalization are in many ways reducing the need for human workers in all types of jobs, although there is contention about how many jobs will be lost to automation. One alarming and frequently cited study of the susceptibility of U.S. jobs to computerization by Frey and Osborne found that as much as 47 percent of U.S. employment may be at risk in the future as a result of computerization and a result of automation.[31] The authors point out that while in the past technological progress resulted in deskilling of some jobs and was oriented towards routine and repetitive tasks, the advent of "big data" means that many nonroutine, more highly skilled jobs requiring significant cognitive ability are now amenable to computerization.

Of course, the Covid-19 pandemic, ongoing at this writing, is likely to change the future of jobs considerably. As economies shut down to deal with the disease, workers who were formerly considered low level or unskilled have gained credence and visibility, including grocery store workers, technicians of all sorts who keep infrastructure running, health care workers, farm workers, delivery and online services, and teachers, to name just a few. Many people who were not out of work altogether began to learn how to work from home. Teaching was being done (when it was being done at all) through distance learning methods, suddenly imposed on instructors with little warning or preparation who then evidenced tremendous creativity in their responses. Or it was being attempted by parents struggling to combine at home work (or unemployment) with getting their children to learn online—no easy task for many. Travel, particularly business travel, largely ceased for the duration of the pandemic, and many people learned how to communicate through online conferencing platforms instead of in person. It is possible that some jobs will now be valued in new ways after the crisis—changing the shape of the future of jobs—as more people recognize how dependent the rest of us are on the work of people in those jobs.

It is not just unskilled or less-skilled jobs at risk—or possibly becoming more valued. Some of the routine aspects of more service-oriented

[31] Frey, C.B., and M.A. Osborne. 2017. "The Future of Employment: How Susceptible are Jobs to Computerisation?" *Technological Forecasting and Social Change 114*, pp. 254–280.

and high-skill work will be done, sometimes better, by computers using various combinations of algorithms, big data, artificial intelligence, and advanced speech recognition software. Among those people whose work is at risk are doctors, lawyers, financial advisors, educators, farmers, drivers of all sorts of vehicles, accountants, and other jobs that used to require human interaction and brainpower to be done effectively. Robotic devices have already displaced many lesser-skilled workers. Expected price declines for such technology will only result in even greater adoption and worker displacement, even in low-wage contexts like China.[32]

Having sufficient jobs for everyone who wants to work and earn an equitable and decent living in the future looks problematic, particularly since it is likely that many businesses shuttered during the pandemic will never reopen. On the other hand, some estimates suggest that millions of new jobs will emerge as a result of artificial intelligence and automation, more than compensating for job losses. Should this more optimistic prediction come true, one serious implication is that more than 50 percent of the workforce will require significantly new skills and training to be able to perform those jobs.[33] The loss of decent and well-paying work for people without advanced technological skills is also important because, for many people, work provides a significant source of meaning and purpose in their lives, something essential to well-being.

Technological and Other Disruptions

As computers' abilities to cope successfully with tasks demanding creativity and social intelligence increase, Frey and Osborne say that "generalist occupations requiring knowledge of human heuristics, and specialist occupations involving the development of novel ideas and artifacts, are the least susceptible to computerization."[34] That is, highly skilled jobs that require understanding of people (emotional intelligence) and creativity

---

[32]   Frey and Osborne, Future of employment.
[33]   World Economic Forum, The Future of Jobs Report. 2018. http://www3.weforum.org/docs/WEF_Future_of_Jobs_2018.pdf (accessed May 26, 2020).
[34]   Frey and Osborne 2017, p. 266.

are at the lowest risk of automation. Managerial, financial, educational, health care, engineering, science, media, and artistic work are probably least likely to succumb to automation.

Along similar lines, the McKinsey Global Institute identified 12 potentially disruptive technologies that will likely affect the nature and availability of work in the future. These technologies include mobile Internet, automation of knowledge work, the Internet of Things, cloud technology, advanced robotics, autonomous and near-autonomous vehicles, next-generation genomics, energy storage, 3D printing, advanced materials, advanced oil and gas exploration and recovery, and renewable energy. They will affect the availability of what the International Labor Organization calls decent work over the coming decades.[35] McKinsey finds that as many as 140 million jobs, mostly knowledge work, could be substituted by algorithms by 2025, although new types of highly sophisticated jobs will likely also be gained in that process. Artificial intelligence (AI), for example, is expected to replace as many as 40 percent of existing jobs by the early 2030s.[36] While AI is also expected to add many jobs, it will likely replace lost jobs with ones requiring much higher skill levels—skills that not many people have, according to *Fortune*.[37]

Offshoring and Outsourcing

Other major factors affecting job availability include offshoring and outsourcing, which are different manifestations of similar phenomena.

---

[35] Mayika, M., M. Chui, J. Bugyhin, R. Dobbs, P. Bisson, and A. Mars. 2013. "Disruptive Technologies: Advances that Will Transform Life, Business, and the Global Economy." McKinsey Global Institute. http://mckinsey.com/business-functions/digital-mckinsey/our-insights/disruptive-technologies (accessed May 26, 2020).

[36] Reisinger, D. 2019. "AI Expert Says Automation Could replace 40% of Jobs in 15 Years." *Fortune*, January 10, 2019, http://fortune.com/2019/01/10/automation-replace-jobs/ (accessed May 26, 2020).

[37] Renaie, R. 2019. "Artificial Intelligence Jobs are on the Rise." *Fortune*, November 29, 2019, http://fortune.com/2018/11/29/ai-jobs-worldwide/ (accessed May 26, 2020).

Outsourcing can mean purchasing goods and services from outside vendors or contracting work out, frequently abroad from the focal nation, to areas where wages tend to be much lower and labor supply greater. Offshoring, which means to base some of a company's manufacturing or service delivery outside of the focal nation where costs are lower, has much the same effect of reducing jobs in the focal nation. The terms are used here interchangeably.

One report suggests that job outsourcing in the United States increases unemployment. Prior to the pandemic, the data suggested that 14.3 million jobs were outsourced, while 5.9 million Americans were unemployed.[38] Among the most popular reasons for outsourcing are cost control, the ability to gain access to resources that are unavailable to companies internally, and the desire to free up internal resources.[39]

Hidden Unemployment

The situation is even more complicated than losses from automation and outsourcing/offshoring suggest. The International Labor Organization estimates a total global workforce of about 3.45 billion, about a third of whom or 1.27 billion are women. That figure suggests that there are about 200 million people unemployed and actively seeking work.[40] Another two billion adults in the world, however, were classified as "outside" the labor force—not employed or looking for employment before the pandemic erased many jobs, which only made the situation worse. As the Overseas Development Institute (ODI) argues in a report on jobs and automation, many of these two billion people might, in fact, work if work

---

[38] Amadeo, K. 2020. "How Outsourcing Jobs Affects the US Economy." *The Balance*, January 25, 2020, https://thebalance.com/how-outsourcing-jobs-affects-the-u-s-economy-3306279 (accessed April 14, 2020).

[39] Statistic Brain. 2017. "Job Overseas Outsourcing Statistics." http://statisticbrain.com/outsourcing-statistics-by-country/ (accessed May 26, 2020).

[40] Gelb, S., and A. Khan. 2013. "Towards a Complete Jobs Picture: A New Lens on Labour Data Gaps and on Automation." London: Overseas Development Institute https://odi.org/sites/odi.org.uk/files/resource-documents/11226.pdf (accessed May 26, 2020).

were available and the majority (about 1.38 billion) are women.[41] Even if losses are less than some hypothesize, however, the ODI report concludes that "What is not in question is that the impact will involve a long-term adjustment, with significant costs for workers in both industrialized and developing countries."[42]

Moving Forward

This chapter has only been able to outline a few of the major forces and trends that affect today's business systems and employees, and, by extension, societies. Numerous other issues could be cited: the dehumanization of many companies' production systems, supply chain issues around how people and the natural environment are treated, for a couple. There is also a clear lack of democracy in most workplaces, with little potential for "voice" in many businesses. There are issues associated with human trafficking, excessive marketing of unnecessary, useless, and even harmful products, not to mention inhumane animal husbandry practices, industrial agriculture that fosters topsoil erosion, overuse of pesticides and human-made fertilizers, among a host of issues. Such problematic practices point to the need for transformation of the socioeconomic and business system—and they do not even account for issues around sustainability, climate change, and exploitation of nature's bounty.

The next chapter explores the socioecological (as opposed to economic) context in which today's businesses and our societies operate. It highlights the systemic risks we as a species are facing—many of which are self-induced. It then attempts to provide a basis for understanding what it will take to stop humanity from driving itself off of that societal and ecological cliff.

The road ahead will not be easy to negotiate, which is why we need to think about transforming the system. There are powerful forces at play that want to keep today's momentum and trajectory on the same path as it has been, without recognizing the need for change. At the same time, it is important to note that there are increasing numbers of people who

---

41   Gelb and Khan, "Towards a Complete Job Picture," 2017.
42   Gelb and Khan, "Towards a Complete Jobs Picture, 2017," p. 8.

already recognize the problems and are willing to work towards transformation and well-being for all, where "all" includes both all humans and the rest of Nature's beings. The rest of the book begins to articulate what that transformation to well-being might look like and how each of us might play our part in moving change or what my late friend Malcolm McIntosh called the "necessary transition"[43] forward.

---

[43] McIntosh, M., ed. 2013. *The Necessary Transition: The Journey Towards the Sustainable Enterprise Economy*. Sheffield, UK: Greenleaf.

CHAPTER 2

Look in the Mirror: Self-Induced Systemic Crises

In the Chapter 1, we explored a few of today's problematic social conditions as they have been shaped by technology and prevailing ideas about what economies and societies are all about. The idea that frames this book is to develop an emerging socioeconomic perspective that is more relational/connected, holistic, dignity-based, and affirmatively life-giving, not just for humans, rather for all living beings and the planet as a whole. Such a perspective serves as the basis of a vision of societies with their embedded economies and associated business practices that are life-(not wealth-) centric, and that foster dignity, well-being in a just and flourishing world for all. Transformation towards these ideas, which for succinctness will be called flourishing for all, is the focus of this book.

Shifting towards flourishing for all involves a process of transformational system change, sooner rather than later given the ecological imperatives outlined below. Some have called this goal of flourishing creating collective value absent dignity violations.[1] In contrast, today's economic and business systems are oriented almost wholly towards economic growth or financial wealth, with much of that wealth going to the already well off. This chapter briefly examines how today's dominant economic system came to be. Understanding that development should help define the kind of transformation needed to shift towards goals of life-affirming well-being, justice, and dignity for all. Later chapters will explore how concepts of transformational system change can help in the change processes sorely needed to deal with the many crises outlined here.

---

[1] Donaldson, T., and J.P. Walsh. 2015. "Toward a Theory of Business." *Research in Organizational Behavior* 35, pp. 181–207.

Flourishing or well-being are encompassing terms that provide for human dignity, and the dignity of other living beings and even the earth itself, conceived as the living system Gaia. Well-being also can include the idea of flourishing societies in which all living entities have places in the natural ecosystems that support those societies. Flourishing ensures that all people have a place where they belong—in homes, communities, organizations, and associations of various types, and societies, where all can live up to their own potential. Where all can earn a decent living and support their families in appropriate ways. Where all experience desired freedoms and where rights that are important are upheld. Where all can exhibit their creativity, integrity, and wholeness, as well as experience an intimate connection with nature. Where all can, in return for what they have been gifted, do their own bit to leave the world a better place for their grandchildren's grandchildren.

Flourishing for *all* also ensures the health and dignity of other living creatures, ecosystems, and the whole of Gaia, the name given to earth conceived as a living system. Dignity, well-being, and flourishing provide the capability for people to live up to their potential and desires as well as being an inherently life-giving activity. Moving in the direction of flourishing for all requires recognition of our interconnectedness with each other and with nature.

A Brief Excursion into Today's Systemic Risks

In some ways, the whole socioeconomic system that we in the developed world have come to know is at risk today. The collapse accompanying the Covid-19 pandemic in health care systems economies, businesses, restaurants, and social supports, to name only a few, and the growing climate emergency demonstrate clearly the fragility of the system that has been built in the so-called developed world in the years following World War II. Simultaneously, many people in developing nations still struggle to make ends meet on a daily basis, especially when their traditional lifestyles and living arrangements have been taken away from them. Particularly important—and threatening—to global well-being are ecological risks that are becoming increasingly well known.

Climate Change and Planetary Boundaries

American scientist Jared Diamond argued in his book *Collapse* that two factors threaten civilizational collapse: pushing ecological resources beyond their capacity to support the relevant population and growing gaps between rich and poor.[2] One other relevant factor related to civilizational collapse identified by Diamond is dysfunctional political and cultural practices. Dysfunctional practices fail to take into account the well-being of all—including nature and her creatures in the interests of the few. Unfortunately, humanity as a whole—and industrial societies in particular—and for the first time on a global scale—now faces all three of these issues.

Both inequality and ecological sustainability are truly global problems at a scope and scale that humanity has never confronted before. For a long time, it was easy to believe that we humans were separate from each other, and from nature. That belief made exploitation—of other people and of nature, the process that many observers call colonialization—easier to tolerate. If "man" is dominant over nature, then practices that strip nature of resources are more justifiable.[3] If some humans are "superior" to others because they have wealth or power, then dehumanizing others who look, act, or live differently becomes easier to do.

These inequitable practices create the instability that can result in serious social unrest. Many places in the world experienced this reality in late 2019, when severe and long-lasting protests emerged in numerous nations of the world against social inequalities. Protests fueled by anger at inequality, lack of voice/democracy, and climate change erupted in places as far apart and distinct as Paris, Zimbabwe, Sudan, Venezuela, Haiti, Iran, Chile, Hong Kong, and Lebanon. Further, the potential for climate change causing collapsing human civilization fueled activities like those

---

[2] Diamond, J. 2005. *Collapse: How Societies Choose to Fail or Succeed*. New York, NY: Penguin.

[3] Riane Eisler lays out the history of what she calls "dominator cultures" in her masterpiece, Eisler, R. 1988. *The Chalice and the Blade: Our History, Our Future*. San Francisco: Harper & Row.

of young climate activist Greta Thunberg[4] and groups like Extinction Rebellion's[5] efforts to bring attention to that civilizational threat.

The global pandemic triggered by rapid spread of Covid-19 infections across the world, the impending global climate change disaster, and all of the social inequalities highlighted by protests, if nothing else, showed how interconnected the world really is. It took only a matter of weeks for the virus to spread around the world, affecting every nation in numerous ways. While in the past various populations in different smaller regions have experienced the types of collapses Diamond studied, this combination of factors highlights the true fragility of today's socioeconomic systems, with their inability to provide broad-based support for the flourishing of all. At scale, humans in the past have had neither the capability nor sufficient numbers, as they now do, to affect the health of the entire planet. Now we do.

Consider: never before in human history has humanity's footprint had the wherewithal to affect climate. Yet that is what the Intergovernmental Panel on Climate Change (IPCC), in consensus documents with which about 97–98 percent of climate scientists concur, agrees is now happening.[6] In a 2014 report that should have been frightening to all but the most ardent climate change deniers, the IPCC argues that "Human influence on the climate system is clear. Recent anthropogenic emissions of greenhouse gases are the highest in history. Recent climate change has already had widespread impacts on human and natural systems."[7]

---

[4]   See Thunberg, G., Wikipedia. 2020. https://en.wikipedia.org/wiki/Greta_Thunberg (accessed April 14, 2020).

[5]   Extinction Rebellion Website. 2020. https://rebellion.earth/ (accessed April 14, 2020).

[6]   IPCC. 2014. "Summary for Policymakers." In *Climate Change 2014: Impacts, Adaptation, and Vulnerability. Part A: Global and Sectoral Aspects. Contribution of Working Group II to the Fifth Assessment Report of the Intergovernmental Panel on Climate Change, eds.* Field, C.B., Barros, V.R., Dokken, D.J., Mach, K.J., Mastrandrea, M.D., Bilir, T.E., Chatterjee, M., Ebi, K.L., Estrada, Y.O., Genova, R.C., Girma, B., Kissel, E.S., Levy, A.N. MacCracken, S. Mastrandrea, P.R. and White, L.L, 1–3. Cambridge and New York,NY: Cambridge University Press.

[7]   IPCC, Summary, p. 2.

Stating that human influence on global warming is "unequivocal," the IPCC notes that since the inception of the industrial era oceans and atmospheres are warming, and many frightening shifts have taken place. While snow and ice (whose albedo effects reflect heat and therefore are cooling influences) are lessening, oceans are acidifying and salinity is shifting, with unprecedented increases in greenhouse gases (GHGs), including carbon dioxide, methane, and nitrous oxide. Extreme weather events have increased as climate change continues, with fewer cold extremes, increases in droughts and extreme heat events, as well as heavy precipitation events, all of which are predicted to intensify over the 21st century. Among other impacts are a reduction in food security, global marine species redistribution, flooding of coastal areas as oceans rise, harm to coral reefs and polar ecosystems, exacerbation of existing human health problems, water shortages, to name a few expected impacts.[8]

Importantly and often unrecognized, not all of the effects of today's GHG emissions are experienced in the near term. As author Bruce Johansen has pointed out, "Global warming is a deceptively backhanded crisis in which thermal inertia delivers results a half-century or more after our burning of fossil fuels provokes them."[9] In other words, as Johansen notes, the GHG effects of fossil fuels we are burning today will take at least 50 years to evidence themselves in the atmosphere and as much as 150 years in the oceans. The implication is stunning for climate change: even if humanity stopped producing excess GHGs today, the effects would be being felt for many decades.[10]

---

[8] IPCC, Summary.

[9] Johansen, B.E. 2016. "Trump's Climate-Change Denial Makes a Miserable Future more Likely." *Newstimes*, November 23, 2016. http://newstimes.com/opinion/article/Bruce-E-Johansen-Trump-s-climate-change-10630865.php, and talk at the Sustainable Wisdom: Integrating Indigenous Knowhow for Global Flourishing conference, University of Notre Dame, September 11–15, 2016.

[10] Also IPCC, Summary, p. 16.

Further, as the IPCC noted and Pope Francis discussed in his 2015 encyclical *Laudato Si'* "Our Common Home,"[11] the poor and the disadvantaged are far more dramatically and negatively affected than more advantaged people. Importantly, humans are not the only living beings affected by climate change and the various sustainability crises facing the planet. The IPCC notes that "a large fraction of species faces increased extinction risk due to climate change."[12] The risk of extinction due to climate change exacerbates an ongoing process of mass extinction that scientists call the sixth great extinction, which threatens as much as three-quarters of the planet's species.[13]

In 2018, the IPCC issued an, if anything, more compelling report that addressed the implications of global warming above 1.5°C, which the IPCC claims as a likely global temperature rise between 2030 and 2052 if significant systemic changes are not made.[14] A key point outlined in this latter report is that such anthropogenic (human-induced) warming will most likely persist for a very long time—the IPCC estimates between centuries to even millennia—wreaking further havoc on humankind. If warming is controlled below 1.5°C, according to the IPCC, that level will be much safer for humanity than a rise to 2.0°C, but will still make human life riskier than we are now experiencing.

---

[11]   Holy Father Pope Francis. 2015. "Encyclical Letter." *Laudato Si': On Care for Our Common Home*. Rome/The Vatican: The Holy See http://w2.vatican.va/content/dam/francesco/pdf/encyclicals/documents/papa-francesco_20150524_enciclica-laudato-si_en.pdf

[12]   IPCC, Summary, p. 13.

[13]   See, for example, Larsen, J. 2004. "The Sixth Great Extinction: Status Report." *Humanist-Buffalo* 64, no. 6, p. 6; Leakey, R., and R. Lewin. 1996. *The Sixth Extinction: Biodiversity and Its Survival*. London: Anchor: Weidenfeld and Nicolson. 1996. And Barnosky, A.D., N. Matzke, S. Tomiya, G.O. Wogan, B. Swartz, T.B. Quental, C. Marshall, J.L. McGuire, E.L., Linsey, K.C. Maguire, B. Mersey, B. and E.A. Ferrer. 2011. "Has the Earth/s Sixth Mass Extinction Already Arrived?" *Nature* 471, no. 7336, pp. 51–57.

[14]   IPCC (Intergovernmental Panel on Climate Change). 2018. Global Warming of 1.5°C: All Chapters. 2018. http://ipcc.ch/report/sr15/ (accessed April 20, 2020).

Since the 2018 IPCC report, other reports have indicated the serious issues in other aspects of the natural environment (beyond human civilizations), including the ongoing extinction of up to a million species report in 2019 by the Intergovernmental Science-Policy Platform on Biodiversity and Ecosystem Services.[15] Further, more than 10,000 scientists signed a "warning" to humanity about what they labeled the climate emergency in 2019,[16] a language echoed by activists like Extinction Rebellion and Greta Thunberg.

The problem is that keeping planetary warming to or below 1.5°C means making significant shifts in emissions in all economic sectors. That reduction needs to be accomplished sooner rather than later. Achieving that goal means decreasing demand for energy and simultaneously lowering emissions from energy and fully "decarbonizing" the electricity sector, removing carbon dioxide from the atmosphere. It means fostering renewables as the key energy source, while balancing land-use practices, bioenergy production, and carbon storage. The key to IPCC is that time is running short before irreversible negative impacts on nature and its biodiversity will occur.

It is clear from the Covid-19 pandemic that other sustainability crises, in addition to climate change, are facing the planet. The Stockholm Resilience Centre has developed what is called the planetary boundaries framework, which identifies nine planetary boundaries that scientists there believe cannot be breached without significant negative consequences to humanity. These boundaries include stratospheric ozone, biodiversity, chemical pollution, climate change, ocean acidification, freshwater consumption, land system change, nitrogen and phosphorus flows in the biosphere and oceans, and atmospheric aerosol loading. Scientists at the

---

[15] Diaz, S., J. Settele, and E. Brondizio. 2019. "Summary for Policymakers of the Global Assessment Report on Biodiversity and Ecosystem Services of the Intergovernmental Science-Policy Platform on Biodiversity and Ecosystem Services." https://ipbes.net/sites/default/files/2020-02/ipbes_global_assessment_report_summary_for_policymakers_en.pdf (accessed May 3, 2020).

[16] Ripple, W.J., C. Wolf, T.M. Newsom, P. Barnard, W.R. Moomaw, and 11258 others. 2019. "World Scientists' Warning of a Climate Emergency." *Bioscience* https://academic.oup.com/bioscience/advance-article/doi/10.1093/biosci/biz088/5610806?searchresult=1 (accessed April 13, 2020).

Centre believe that four of these boundaries have already been crossed (one of two of the biosphere integrity indicators, deforestation, atmospheric carbon dioxide, and the flow of nitrogen and phosphorus), with several others close to being transgressed.[17] As the many scientists involved in the project note, "Transgressing one or more planetary boundaries may be deleterious or even catastrophic due to the risk of crossing thresholds that will trigger non-linear, abrupt environmental change within continental-to planetary-scale systems."[18]

Although Resilience Centre scientists initially framed their study as preliminary, their findings have been updated and are now widely recognized as offering important benchmarks for "new thinking on global sustainability."[19] The scientists claim that there is an "urgent need for a new paradigm that integrates the continued development of human societies and the maintenance of the earth system (ES) in a resilient and accommodating state," as a 2015 update puts it.[20]

Ecological/Sustainability Crises

To think that climate change is the only existential crisis facing humanity that results from both the growth in population of human beings on the planet (projected by the United Nations to reach approximately 8.6 billion people by 2030 and 9.8 billion by 2050, assuming no disastrous collapse) would be to be seriously mistaken. Humanity's growth and exploitative practices are already pressuring many ecosystems as a result

---

[17]   Stockholm Resilience Centre, Four of nine planetary boundaries now crossed. 2015. https://www.su.se/english/about/news-and-events/press/press-releases/four-of-nine-planetary-boundaries-now-crossed-1.218003 (accessed May 26, 2020).

[18]   J. Rockström, W.L. Steffen, K. Noone, A. Persson, F.S. Chapin III, E. Lambin, E., et al., 2009. "Planetary Boundaries: Exploring the Safe Operating Space for Humanity." *Ecology & Society* 14, no. 2, 32, http://ecologyandsociety.org/vol14/iss2/art32/

[19]   Rockström, et al., Planetary boundaries, abstract.

[20]   Steffen, W., K. Richardson, J. Rockström, S.E. Cornell, I. Fetzer, E.M. Bennett, R. Biggs, et al. 2015. "Planetary Boundaries: Guiding Human Development on a Changing Planet." *Science* 347, no. 6223, 1259855–10.

of what is called the Great Acceleration, which has pushed our climate into a new era known as the Anthropocene.

The Anthropocene or era of human activity influencing climate and the natural environment, so labeled by Paul Crutzen,[21] places human activity right in the center of climatic changes. Such changes have become markedly more apparent since about 1950 through a serious of charts (hockey stick–shaped charts) that show rapid acceleration in problematic socioeconomic and earth systems arenas. On the socioeconomic side are trends in global population, real gross domestic product (GDP), energy use, fertilizer consumption, and urban population, among others. The earth system trends show significant, negatively impactful, changes in a broad array of areas including increased carbon dioxide (associated with global warming), nitrous oxide, methane, stratospheric ozone, surface temperature, ocean acidification, tropical forest loss, and domesticated land, among others.[22] (Note: These charts can be found at The Anthropocene website: http://anthropocene.info/great-acceleration.php).

In 2018, the World Wildlife Organization (WWF) published a stunning report that details the many ways in which the natural systems that support and give life to human systems are endangered. Except where noted, this section draws from that report, which urgently calls for a "new global deal for nature and people" that would reflect more life-affirming approaches than the current system provides.[23] The WWF report pointed out that the "services," sometimes called ecosystem services, provided by nature are estimated to be as much as $125 trillion annually. The 2020 Future Earth Report similarly highlighted the many crises facing humanity if business as usual continues without needed transformation in arenas

---

[21] Crutzen, P.J. 2006. "Geology of Mankind—The Anthropocene." *Nature* 415, p. 23; Crutzen, P.J. 2006. "The 'Anthropocene,'" In *Earth System Science in the Anthropocene*, 13–19. Springer: Berlin Heidelberg.

[22] For the charts and background information, see Global IGBP (International Geosphere-Biosphere Program) Change, URL: http://igbp.net/globalchange/gre atacceleration.4.1b8ae20512db692f2a680001630.html (accessed May 2, 2019).

[23] WWF, *Living Planet Report—2018: Aiming Higher*. Grooten, M., and R.E.A. Almond, eds. 2018. https://c402277.ssl.cf1.rackcdn.com/publications/1187/ files/original/LPR2018_Full_Report_Spreads.pdf

as sweeping as the climate, politics, ocean management, migration, biodiversity, finance, food, and digital innovation.[24]

One major threat to the future health of the planet, and of humans, is biodiversity loss. The world is now said to be undergoing what is known as the sixth great extinction, with massive losses of biodiversity annually, caused (as is climate change) by human activities.[25] WWF points out graphically that "All our economic activity ultimately depends on nature," and that the Living Planet Index documents a species population decline of 60 percent between 1970 and 2014.[26]

Biodiversity, according to the WWF, is threatened by a number of human activities, including excessive consumption of natural resources, growth of use of products associated with deforestation. Deforestation in turn threatens wildlife, conversion of land to agricultural uses, which disrupts habitats and pollution. Reductions in the number of bees and other pollinators, which account for pollinating about 87 percent of flowering plants, and degradation of topsoil, particularly what is known as "living soil," or soil rich with life forms, which is at major risk globally, are also significant problems. Importantly, a 2019 report on species extinction indicates that as many as a million species are now at risk because of human activities.[27]

---

[24] Scrutton, A., ed. 2020. "Our Future on Earth Report." *Future Earth*, https://futureearth.org/publications/our-future-on-earth/ (accessed May 26, 2020).

[25] Leakey, R.E., and R. Lewin. 1995. *The Sixth Extinction: Patterns of Life and the Future of Humankind*. New York, NY: Doubleday. Also Eldredge, N. 2001. "The Sixth Extinction, An Action Bioscience.org original article." *American Institute of Biological Sciences* http://endangeredink.com/programs/population_and_sustainability/extinction/pdfs/Eldridge-6th-extinction.pdf (accessed May 26, 2020) and Larsen, J. 2004. "The Sixth Great Extinction: A Status Report." *The Humanist* 64, no. 6, 6–6, http://earth-policy.org/plan_b_updates/2004/update35 (accessed May 26, 2020).

[26] WWF, Living Planet Report, p. 10.

[27] Diaz, S., J. Settele, and E. Brondizio. 2019. "Summary for Policymakers of the Global Assessment Report on Biodiversity and Ecosystem Services of the Intergovernmental Science-Policy Platform on Biodiversity and Ecosystem Services." *IPBES* https://ipbes.net/sites/default/files/2020-02/ipbes_global_assessment_report_summary_for_policymakers_en.pdf

Biodiversity loss is only one of many ecological threats. Others include invasive species invasions, overexploitation resulting from deforestation and agricultural practices, which themselves are associated with what WWF calls "runaway consumption," which is eroding the planet's biocapacity. And, of course, we all learned with the pandemic in 2020 about the transfer of uncontrollable diseases from animals to humans. Biocapacity is the ability of a biological system to regenerate and renew itself, as well as absorb wastes. When biocapacity is exceeded the human ecological footprint is more than the renewal ability of a given ecosystem. The result is an unsustainable ecosystem. WWF notes that although biocapacity has actually increased, it has fallen behind human populations' ecological footprint.

WWF highlights steep declines in ocean habitats that are important to human welfare, including coral reefs, which support about a fourth of marine life and have already been diminished by about half, and mangroves, which both sequester carbon and provide a home for many ocean species, are also greatly deteriorated, along with other important ocean ecosystems. Similarly, global fisheries are being overexploited, with the result that annual fish catch is decreasing rapidly. Ocean health is also threatened by growing concentrations of plastic waste, especially from single-use plastics, used once and discarded only to end up in massive oceanic swirls along with other human debris. Such waste is particularly problematic because ocean animals eat it—thinking it is food, or get trapped in plastic bags or other remnants that end up in oceanic waters. Many fisheries are also at risk of collapse because of overly zealous fishing practices.

Forests are another important area of concern, because of their capacity for storing carbon and producing oxygen. Forests also provide numerous so-called ecosystem services, as WWF points out, including protecting watersheds, reducing erosion, providing shelter and habitats for animals, insects, and other living beings, and helping to mitigate climate change.

Topsoil and land suited to agriculture have been degraded by industrial farming practices and overuse, with accompanying significant reductions in the population of bees and other insects that pollinate plants. The importance of life *in* the dirt or soil is often overlooked, yet as much as a quarter of all of the Earth's living beings can be found in soil. Studies reported by WWF suggest that there is a clear link between human population and activity (like agriculture, urbanization, pollution) and degraded life in soils, including decreasing insect populations. The reason that biodiversity in soils is important is that living organisms in the soil are foundational to ecosystem processes like carbon and other greenhouse gas sequestration, and nutrient uptake by plants, not to mention specific uses by humans of the variety of organisms in the soil.

The 2019 report from the Intergovernmental Science-Policy Platform on Biodiversity (IPBES) mentioned earlier puts the biodiversity situation in ever more stark terms.[28] As noted above, IPBES warned of unprecedented and accelerating levels of species extinction, with up to a million species at risk of extinction. The report called for transformative changes in human systems so that natural systems can be protected and restored to health. IPBES found that land-based habitats have fallen by about 20 percent since 1900, and that as much as 40 percent of amphibian and 33 percent of reef-forming coral species are at risk. And that is the tip of the iceberg: insect populations, vertebrate species, and even domesticated animals are all threatened. As one of the authors of the report, Prof. Joseph Settele, put it, "Ecosystems, species, wild populations, local varieties and breeds of domesticated plants and animals are shrinking, deteriorating or vanishing. The essential, interconnected web of life on Earth is getting smaller and increasingly frayed. The loss is a direct result of human activity and constitutes a direct threat to human well-being in all regions of the world."[29]

Dysfunctional Political and Cultural Practices

As to the third civilizational threat identified by Diamond, dysfunctional political and cultural practices, one needs only to look at the dysfunction caused by the Brexit vote in the UK. Or the divisiveness created by the election of populist leaders in numerous countries around the globe

---

[28]   S. Diaz, J. Settele, and E. Brondizio, 2019. "Summary."
[29]   Quoted in IPBES Media Release. 2019. "Nature's Dangerous Decline 'Unprecedented' Species Extinction Rates 'Accelerating,'" https://ipbes.net/news/Media-Release-Global-Assessment (accessed May 26, 2020).

(including the United States), and the inequality generated by today's economic system. Or the total disruption of what was thought to be normal by the Covid-19 pandemic. Protests by citizens around the world, many triggered in 2019, are evidence of growing unease with today's approaches to societies and economies and problem solving within them. Protests, which were tamped down by the Covid-19 outbreak, also speak to the lack of progress in many places on huge issues like inequality, climate change, jobs and meaningful work, and poverty, problems greatly exacerbated by the pandemic.

Lack of trust in major institutions in society—like governments and businesses—has grown rapidly in the 21st century, particularly with the Global Financial Crisis of 2007–2008 and in its aftermath, when too little seemed to change. Angry citizens have often voted against their own self-interest in the name of change for change's sake. Politicians seem unable to cooperate or collaborate around important public issues or in the public interest, instead (in the United States, anyway) being bought out by major donors through political action committees that contribute without restrictions—or consequences. In the United States, there are now periodic government shutdowns or partial shutdowns because no agreement can be reached on budgets—or for other, more political and equally dysfunctional—reasons. Uprisings and migrations from abusive, hostile situations have created a global crisis around migration, as people flee from their homes in the hope of finding a better life, only to find that there are few places for them to go. Such migration and the presence of refugees living marginal lives will only worsen if climate change proceeds unabated, as about 40 percent of people globally now live in coastal urban areas most threatened by rising seas.

The annual trust survey (called a barometer) by Edelman 2019 indicated that only 20 percent of people globally believed that the system was working for them.[30] Additionally, that survey found that people now trusted their employers (75 percent) to do what is right more than NGOs

---

[30]   Edelman Trust Barometer. 2019. URL: https://edelman.com/sites/g/files/aatuss191/files/2019-03/2019_Edelman_Trust_Barometer_Global_Report.pdf?utm_source=website&utm_medium=global_report&utm_campaign=downloads (accessed May 26, 2020).

(57 percent), businesses (56 percent), or the media (47 percent).[31] Trust in business rose in 2019 despite the reality that the same survey reveals that the majority of employees fear job loss resulting from lack of training and skills for the jobs available, automation, and international conflicts about trade and tariffs, with the fears being highest for employees of multinational firms. Despite increases in trust for governments globally overall in 20 of 26 markets studied by Edelman, overall trust in government remained at 47 percent.[32]

The Edelman Trust Barometer in 2020 indicated that inequality—a sense of inequity in the system—was undermining trust in all of these societal institutions.[33] The majority of people believed that today's capitalism did more harm than good in the world (56 percent) and that the vast majority of employees feared losing their jobs (83 percent). At this writing, it is too soon to know how the fact that governments all around the world were forced to intervene strongly during the pandemic—and provide (or fail to provide) social supports will impact peoples' views of government for the long term. Certainly, the disruptions caused by the pandemic create a situation in which many people are forced to recognize that continually stripping governments of their ability to provide some sort of social safety net—and has happened since the 1980s under the banner of neoliberalism—may not always be the best strategy.

There is plenty of other evidence of dysfunctional practices and cultures, including overconsumption patterns, food "products" with high salt, fat, and sugar contents that contribute to a growing obesity crisis globally, excessive focus on financial wealth to the exclusion of values that matter, poor distribution of the world's food, which leaves many people hungry and malnourished, and many others. Add in the impact of social media, both for good in connecting people, and for problematic reasons, in putting forward unrealistic standards. Sometimes social media (inadvertently?) foments messaging that undermines democratic processes and generates more divisiveness and other problems. One could also note

---

[31] 2019 Edelman Trust Barometer, 1.
[32] 2019 Edelman Trust Barometer, 1.
[33] 2020 Edelman Trust Barometer. 2020. URL: https://edelman.com/trustbarometer (accessed April 4, 2020).

falling trust in the fourth estate (the press), as noted by the Edelman 2019 survey, some parts of which are failing to maintain their legitimate role as arbiter of the truth. Failing infrastructure in many nations is also a manifestation of dysfunction, as highways and public transportation systems erode, bridges collapse, and other aspects of the infrastructure necessary for modern societies to function well weaken.

Growing inequality also poses a significant set of risks. The Institute for Policy Studies' Inequality.org website highlights the fact that inequality has been growing globally decades with the world's richest 1 percent of the population now holding some 45 percent of global wealth. In that same context, the "ultra-rich" (i.e., individuals who hold more than $30 million) hold some 11.3 percent of total wealth as of 2019 but are 0.0003 percent of global population. Oxfam's 2019 report indicated that 26 billionaires held as much wealth as the world's poorest 3.8 billion people.[34] Since Jared Diamond in his book *Collapse* cited growing gaps between rich and poor as one of the significant civilizational destabilizers, clearly this situation is untenable over the long term—and perhaps even over the shorter term, given the notable protests of 2019.

Off a Cliff?

The situation described above has complicated causes, of course, and many other important issues might be raised. The key point is that the trajectory for humanity, according to climate scientists in particular, is not good. As Diamond's work points out, sustainability issues, climate change, and growing inequality, along with dysfunctional practices, pose civilization-threatening risks to humanity. Add in the political divisiveness of the current era, terrorism, the refugee crisis, issues around cybersecurity, artificial intelligence, the Covid-19 pandemic and the potential for others, and privacy issues associated with what scholar Shoshana Zuboff

---

[34] Quackenbush, C. 2019. "The World's Top 26 Billionaires Now Own as Much as the Poorest 3.8 Billion, Says Oxfam." *Time*, January 21, 2019, https://time.com/5508393/global-wealth-inequality-widens-oxfam/ (accessed May 26, 2020).

calls "surveillance capitalism."[35] Consider also growing civil unrest and an apparent deterioration of democracy, the potential for collapsing ecosystems, massive swirls of plastic waste in our oceans, extreme weather events, and on and on, to include other factors too numerous to detail without creating the impression that little can be done to move forward towards a better world. Elected officials in many places seem overwhelmed by all of these (and other) problems—and unable to come together around an agenda for moving the system to a better place.

The growing reality is that humanity is about to drive itself off a socioecological cliff—in the interests of continued economic "growth" that satisfies mostly the already wealthy. That is why we all need new pathways to flourishing—to a better future. In the next chapter, we look at some of the roots of today's systemic crises. Then we will begin thinking about how systems as complex as our socioecological and socioeconomic systems might be able to transform. The idea is to try to determine how both the human project and other life on the planet can potentially cope with some of today's challenges and learn how to thrive well into the future.

---

[35]   Zuboff, S. 2019. *The Age of Surveillance Capitalism: The Fight for a Human Future at the New Frontier of Power*. London: Profile Books.

CHAPTER 3

Neoliberalism and the Need for Transformation

Here we consider the role of today's dominant economic narrative—neoliberalism in fomenting the crises discussed in Chapter 2.

How Neoliberalism Came to Dominate the World

Today's economic paradigm links with the era of the Enlightenment. The Enlightenment in many ways seems to have severed humans' embeddedness with the notion of a higher power (or even universal consciousness), society, and nature. The philosophy of Descartes (with the notion that "I think, therefore I am") also severed connections within people with the distinction separating mind and body. In the late 20th century, the proponents of neoliberalism, possibly without intending to do so, also severed the market from enhancement of human dignity and flourishing for all, making the market and wealth creation the ultimate goal of societies—rather than somehow serving the public good/interest.

The economy as we know it today had its beginnings in the industrial era with the burgeoning use of fossil fuels starting in the 19th century and, ultimately, the growth of large corporations. In the early days of industrialization, planetary resources seemed boundless; there was plenty of room for human population and resource usage to grow. Today, however, human population has (significantly) more than quadrupled since 1900 to around 7.4 billion people. The United Nations projects human population to reach 8.5 billion by 2030 and 9.7 billion by 2050, assuming trends before the pandemic continue unabated. Globally, human uses of raw materials and ecosystem resources like topsoil, fish in the ocean, forest products, minerals, and too many other natural resources to mention have pushed the earth beyond its capacity for renewal. That reality puts human civilization at risk, as pushing beyond the ecological environment's renewal capacity along with growing gaps between rich and poor are known causes of civilizational collapse.[1]

As French economist Thomas Piketty has demonstrated, however, even in the industrial era most economies were not expected to grow very much, if at all.[2] After World War II, however, the mantra of economic growth at almost any cost took hold, and consumerism with all of its material and resource costs took hold of the public imagination as people struggled to recover from World War II. The tenets of neoliberalism—individual but not shared responsibility, limited government, free trade and free markets, deregulation, an unwillingness to recognize public goods or even the public good, fostering of intense business competition, privatization, and growth at any cost in a society where winners take all—were deliberately promulgated by economists and policymakers. The framers of what we know as the neoliberal agenda or capitalism, so dominant today, brought significant system change about quite deliberately. They created a new cultural mythology around growth, free markets, and individual but not shared responsibilities. They discounted the importance of society and ignored impacts of doing business on the natural environment entirely.

How did it happen? Shortly after World War II, a group of mostly young economists, historians, and philosophers met at what became the Mont Pelerin Society[3] in Mont Pelerin, Switzerland, to discuss what they perceived as a threat to freedom, particularly to free enterprise.[4] Led by well-known economists like Ludwig von Mises and Friedrich Hayek, the

---

[1]   Diamond, J. 2005. *Collapse: How Societies Choose to Fail or Succeed*. New York: Penguin.

[2]   Piketty, T. 2014. *Capital in the Twenty-First Century*. Cambridge, MA: Harvard University Press.

[3]   For background, go to the Mont Pelerin Society, https://montpelerin.org/ (accessed May 26, 2020).

[4]   Ecologist Hunter Lovins pointed to the Mont Pelerin manifesto in framing an entity called Leading for Wellbeing, which ultimately became WEAll, the Wellbeing Economy Alliance. See Wellbeing-Economy Alliance (WEAll) brochure. 2019. https://wellbeingeconomy.org/wp-content/uploads/2019/03/WEAll-brochure_INEdits_Final2.0.pdf (accessed April 13, 2020).

Mont Pelerin group felt that the New Deal that the U.S. Congress passed during President Franklin Roosevelt's administration to ease the impacts of the Great Depression, and the social democracy that was arising across Europe, posed grave threats to freedom, particularly freedom of markets and companies.[5]

Over the course of ten days, this group drew up a "Statement of Aims"[6] or manifesto that articulated the perceived threat and created a set of what framers termed "valid ideals" that fostered the preeminence of private property, competitive free markets and free trade, with reduced or diminished power and roles for government. Highlighting individual freedom and responsibilities, with a particular set of "detailed agreements," the Mont Pelerin Society forwarded an agenda of laudable aims: freedom of thought and expression, rule of law, freedom of the market, and harmonious international relations that they believed would "contribute to the preservation and improvement of the free society."[7]

These economists and others expanded this agenda by founding a number of think tanks to foster neoliberal ideas. As Monbiot details

The movement's rich backers funded a series of think tanks, which would refine and promote the ideology. Among them were the American Enterprise Institute, the Heritage Foundation, the Cato Institute, the Institute of Economic Affairs, the Centre for Policy Studies, and the Adam Smith Institute. They also financed academic positions and departments, particularly at the universities of Chicago and Virginia.[8] These think tanks and academic departments encouraged adoption of neoliberal ideas, which in the US became better known as neoclassical economics. The most ardent and outspoken proponent of this perspective was the University

---

[5] Monbiot, G. 2016. "Neoliberalism—The Ideology at the Root of All of our Problems." *The Guardian*, URL: https://theguardian.com/books/2016/apr/15/neoliberalism-ideology-problem-george-monbiot, (accessed May 26, 2020).

[6] Pelerin, M. 1947. "Society Website, Statement of Aims." https://montpelerin.org/statement-of-aims/ (accessed May 26, 2020).

[7] Mont Pelerin Society website, Statement of Aims.

[8] George Monbiot, Neoliberalism.

of Chicago's economist Milton Friedman, who famously argued in the words of the *New York Times* headline, "The Social Responsibility of Business is to Increase its Profits."[9]

Further enhancing the spread of neoliberalism with its economistic tenets was a chilling, confidential memorandum written by (then) future Supreme Court Justice Walter Powell in 1971 to Eugene B. Sydnor, then Chairman of the Education of Committee of the U.S. Chamber of Commerce.[10] Now called the Powell Memorandum, this document provided a clear roadmap for promulgating the ideas associated with neoliberalism. Arguing that the American economic system was "under broad attack," Powell outlined a series of steps that proponents of neoliberalism needed to take to deal with that attack.

First, Powell argued[11] that the attacks were coming from "Communists, New Leftists, and other revolutionaries who would destroy the entire system, college campuses, the pulpit, the media, the intellectual and literary journals, the arts and sciences, and from politicians." He noted that the response to the attacks from business was, if it existed at all, one of "appeasement, ineptitude and ignoring the problem." To cope, Powell argued that companies needed to appoint executives responsible for "counter[ing]-on the broadest front—the attack on the enterprise system." He then argued that the Chamber of Commerce, to whom the memo was addressed, needed to use its resources to undertake long-term planning over an indefinite period of time, using the combined resources of many firms to fight the "attacks," as doing so would take attention away from any one corporation's efforts in that regard.

To deal with the perceived threats from "the campus," Powell advocated for creating "balance" in perspectives, which he thought absent

---

[9]   Milton, M.F. 1970. "The Social Responsibility of a Business is to increase its Profits." In *The New York Times Magazine*, pp. 122–24.

[10]   Powell, L.F. 1971. "Confidential Memorandum: Attack of American Free Enterprise System." URL: http://reclaimdemocracy.org/powell_memo_lewis/ (accessed May 26, 2020).

[11]   All quotes in these three paragraphs are from the Powell Memorandum, cited above, unless otherwise noted.

since relatively few conservatives appeared to be present on most campuses. To counter this absence, Powell suggested—and neoliberals later implemented—creating a "staff of scholars" who "believe in the system," with "national reputation whose authorship would be widely respected—even when disagreed with." This staff of scholars would be supplemented by a "staff of speakers of the highest competency" supported by a Speakers Bureau comprised of "the ablest and most effective advocates from the top echelons of American business." In addition, the ideas of neoliberalism were to be inserted into economics, political science, and sociology textbooks on an ongoing basis to "restor[e] the balance essential to genuine academic freedom."

Today, instead of that balance, it would be hard to find an economics textbook that does not focus centrally on the neoliberal ideas of neoclassical economics. (It should be noted that since the 2007–2008 Global Financial Crisis, behavioral economists have made some marginal inroads to counter this dominance. Further, there are student-led movements to create more balanced and realistic economics. In addition, the pandemic has further raised thinking about the assumptions that go into the neoliberal framework.) Powell also stated that the Chamber should insist on "equal time on campus" for conservative ideas and "balancing of faculties."

Powell also argued that business schools could "train" executives by indoctrinating them with these ideas. Secondary education, public opinion, television, other media, and scholarly journals along with all other forms of written work, including advertisements, and politics were not to be left out of this campaign to get the ideas of neoliberalism embedded. Indeed, today, they seem much like the very air that we breathe, such that we can hardly recognize that we are living in an ideology, that is, a story or narrative. That narrative, as may be obvious, was quite deliberately constructed to forward the particular agenda of enterprises or corporations,[12] as opposed to people, life itself, or other living beings. It fosters a growth-at-all costs economic agenda, much to the exclusion of other considerations important to overall well-being, flourishing, or even life itself.

---

[12] Monbiot, Neoliberalism, for a good synthesis of how these ideas spread.

Following the imperatives outlined in the Powell Memorandum, neo-liberals forwarded their agenda, gaining a big boost for their ideas with election of Ronald Reagan in the United States and Margaret Thatcher in the United Kingdom in 1980. (They gained perhaps an even bigger boost with the election of Donald Trump in the United States in 2016 and Boris Johnson in the UK in 2019, as well as other populist leaders in different nations elected during the same period.) Both the United States and the United Kingdom began to implement extreme forms of the neoliberal agenda after 1980. George Monbiot, writing in *The Guardian*, noted that with Reagan and Thatcher's election, "the rest of the package soon followed: massive tax cuts for the rich, the crushing of trade unions, deregulation, privatization, outsourcing and competition in public services." In addition, neoliberal policies were implemented through powerful global actors like the International Monetary Fund, the World Bank, and the World Trade Organization[13] under pressure from the United States and the United Kingdom.

Today's extreme form of neoliberalism or economism has, as Monbiot notes, become more strident,[14] resulting in corporate monopolies, and "efficiency" agendas that allow large corporations and their supply chains to externalize—or throw out into society and the natural environment—many of the costs of production. The real costs of doing business are not counted in today's economic statistics, in part because of these externalities, as economists call them, though the costs are very real to societies and nature. Externalities are defined as the consequences or side-effects of business (or any other) activities that affect people or the natural environment who are considered not part of the production system.

Externalities can be positive or negative, but the most consequential ones are negative. Pollution is a classic negative externality associated with manufacturing, though there are many others, both ecological and societal. Consider, for instance, the negative societal impacts on workers paid very low wages, who work in very poor conditions and are left stranded when companies determine that they can pay even lower wages elsewhere, or during the pandemic when many businesses simply shuttered their

---

13   Monbiot, Neoliberalism.
14   Monbiot, Neoliberalism.

operations without regard for the impact on employees. Think about the negative impacts of overconsumption that leaves many citizens in developed nations feeling more like consumers than citizens and erodes democracy. Reflect on the ecological consequences associated with many manufacturing and agricultural practices left out of product costs, and the inhumane treatment of many animals in industrial farming operations so that "efficiency" can be gained. All are negative externalities of today's growth—and efficiency-oriented production systems, which fail to take broader considerations of flourishing into account.

In the *Sorcerer's Apprentice* and in the novel *Frankenstein*, the inventors lost control of their invention. Similarly, we are currently in a situation, where the laudable goals of the Mont Pelerin Society of protecting dignity and ensuring freedom have largely been lost. The economic system is, in a sense, out of control and not serving human needs. Markets, which were supposed to establish competitive and level-playing fields, have been hijacked by large corporations in the name of freedom, with many goods needed for the public privatized. Corporations in the United States have been granted the same rights to "free speech" that individuals have by the U.S. Supreme Court, despite that they have far more power or clout than do most individuals—and tend to use that money to "support" politicians, thereby buying their loyalty. Stanford Professor Jeffrey Pfeffer points out how much the current corporate setup also hurts employees. In one survey, 61 percent of employees said that workplace stress had made them sick and 7 percent said they had actually been hospitalized.[15] In addition, many consumer products frequently do not enhance peoples' well-being, including high-fructose sodas, high-fat fast foods, and salt-laden snacks designed to hit people's "bliss point" and encourage greater consumption.[16] There is also an imbalance in the distribution of food that shows up as further inequity. The result is an obesity crisis in wealthy, "developed" countries, while people go hungry in still-developing nations.

---

[15] For more background on this research, see Goh, J., Pfeffer, J., and Zenios, S.A. 2016. "The Relationship Between Workplace Stressors and Mortality and Health Costs in the United States." *Management Science* 62, no. 2, pp. 608–28.

[16] Moss, M. 2013. *Salt, Sugar, Fat: How the Food Giants Hooked us.* New York: Random House.

Shifting the system away from what is so familiar towards new ways of conceiving the economy's place in the world is an incredibly difficult and complex process. As must be obvious, the ideas and systems of neoliberalism combined with the ideas of the Enlightenment are deeply embedded in our psyches, systems, norms, and values. Shifting to a broader perspective in which the flourishing of all—including other creatures and nature itself, a valuing of life itself, in fact—is a daunting task. Still, many people must tackle this task if humanity is to thrive in the future.

It is to system transformation that we now turn. To begin with, we explore some ideas about how system transformation happens, then consider whether and how purposeful system transformation might occur towards a life-centered way of being, particularly in the wake of the Covid-19 pandemic. Then, in the next two chapters, we begin an "imaginary" about what a future in which dignity and flourishing—a life-centric socioeconomic orientation—might look like and how we each can do our bit to get there.

System Transformation

Given the many ills noted above—and many more that could be discussed—it is important to begin to imagine what an alternative to today's socioeconomic and ecological systems might be. Ultimately, achieving an alternative vision requires engaging in a process of system transformation that includes many stakeholders, many different types of organizations, operating collaboratively and independently at different levels of society, and working on a wide range of issues. A good portion of these stakeholders will need to gain some sort of broad agreement about the vision of the future—and the new stories that will underpin that future. Only then, arguably, will core aspects of the system that I have elsewhere labeled purposes, perspectives, performance metrics, power distribution, and practices (including operating practices, policies, processes, and procedures) sufficiently change.[17]

---

[17]   Waddock, S. 2020. "Achieving Sustainability Requires Systemic Business Transformation." *Global Sustainability* 3, no. 312, 1–12, URL: https://doi. org/10.1017/sus2020.9 (accessed May 26, 2020).

Further, it is important to understand that system transformation takes place in a context of complexity, which is to say that systems are complex adaptive systems with all the characteristics and attributes of complexity. In addition, socioeconomic systems (and ecological systems) of all sorts can readily be characterized as having what are known as wicked problems—problems that are interdependent, dynamics, interactive, and inherently complex.[18] These characteristics will be explored in more depth below, however, they mean that system change, particularly in a desired direction can never be easy or predictable.

Despite its apparently laudable goals, the neoliberal agenda now operates in such an extreme way that it had increasingly become clear to many observers that transformative change was needed even before the devastation—economic and social—wrought by the Covid-19 pandemic. For one thing, the climate change and sustainability crises combined demand significant transformative change because of the civilization-threatening risks they pose. It is because the impacts of today's way of organizing our economy—and making the *economy*, rather than, say, community/relationships, beauty, life itself, or the common good, central to our existence, that we need transformation. Thus, whatever changes a "new economy" envisions need to incorporate values that, for example, rest on principles that foster life and flourishing in human and natural environments and ensure that communities at all levels and of all types thrive.

Human organizations, communities, whole societies, and natural ecosystems (for brevity, we can call these systems socioeconomic or socioecological systems depending on the focus) are constantly changing. Change is a constant dynamic in living systems of all sorts. Change is particularly notable in healthy systems, which thrive because of the abundance and diversity of elements within them, embodying a set of principles that scholar Andreas Weber calls "enlivenment."[19]

---

[18]   Waddock, S., D. Dentoni, G. Meszoely, and S. Waddell. 2015. "The Complexity of Wicked Problems in Large System Change." *Journal of Organizational Change Management* 28, no. 6, pp. 993–1012.

[19]   Weber, A. 2013. *Enlivenment. Towards a Fundamental Shift in the Concepts of Nature, Culture and Politics.* Berlin: Heinrich-Böll-Stiftung http://autor-andreas-weber.de/downloads/Enlivenment_web.pdf (accessed May 26, 2020).

Since we live inside today's system, it is difficult to gain the perspective necessary to "see" the system—unless of course something like the Covid-19 pandemic highlights how the world is operating. One thing that the pandemic clearly showed is that the world today is highly interconnected, much as physicists have been saying is the case at the quantum level. With the pandemic, it is also easier to see connections between, for example, how the economic system is operating and poverty, as people are laid off without adequate resources as backup, as companies collapse without access to supply chains, and as food systems are threatened because workers cannot work, just as examples.

In fact, one consequence of the pandemic is that many people around the world now recognize the need for system transformation to bring about a better world. That recognition creates an opportunity that might not have otherwise existed, because there is nothing like a crisis to focus people's attention on what really matters.

Living systems such as societies, communities, families, and natural ecologies constantly exhibit "normal" or incremental change. Such change generally tends to go unnoticed, because we all are deeply embedded in the system. Crisis overturns that incrementalism. Crisis creates sometimes chaotic change, while simultaneously drawing attention to what I have pointed to as "cracks" in the system.[20] Indeed, the idea that cracks in the system can be helpful was articulated by the master songwriter Leonard Cohen in his wonderful song called *Anthem*, with the words "There's a crack in everything. That's where the light gets in."[21]

Systems Context of Complexity and Wickedness

Once we begin to see how the current system operates and the broad outlines of its failings, the need to get from today's system with its emphasis on growth, materialism, and the economy at the expense of just about

---

[20]   Waddock, S. 2020. "There's a Crack in Everything. That's Where the Light Gets in." URL: http://one.aom.org/covid-19-insights-from-business-sustainability-scholars/covid-19-insights-waddock (accessed April 16, 2020).

[21]   See the YouTube video of Leonard Cohen singing Anthem in 2008 at : https://youtube.com/watch?v=6wRYjtvIYK0 (accessed April 16, 2020).

everything else, towards a new system that values flourishing life for all becomes evident. (Of course, this need for a holistic perspective has long been evident to Indigenous thinkers[22] and many people in the global South and East,[23] to be discussed later.)

Transformative system change involves socioecological systems that have two important characteristics: (1) they are complex adaptive systems and (2) they are fraught with wicked problems.[24] The interesting thing is that both complexity and wickedness have similar characteristics.

Systems are integrated, interdependent functioning "wholes" that cannot be broken apart of they lose their functioning.[25] Systems are often comprised of other systems—subsystems—operating in nested layers that Arthur Koestler called "holons,"[26] entities that are simultaneously parts of something larger and whole in themselves.

Complexity and Wickedness

Thinking about systems means viewing things holistically rather than breaking them into their parts. Viewed holistically, many systems are what Arthur Koestler called holons.[27] Holons are wholes that are comprised of

[22]   Four Arrows aka Donald Trent Jacobs. 2016. *Point of Departure: Returning to Our More Authentic Worldview for Education and Survival.* Charlotte, NC: IAP.

[23]   See, for example, Chen, M.J. 2002. "Transcending Paradox: The Chinese 'Middle Way' Perspective." *Asia Pacific Journal of Management 19*, nos. 2–3, pp. 179–99, and Chen, M.J., and D. Miller. 2011. "The Relational Perspective as a Business Mindset: Managerial Implications for East and West." *Academy of Management Perspectives 25*, no. 3, pp. 6–18.

[24]   For elaboration of the foundations of large system change as complex adaptive systems fraught with wicked problems, see Waddock, S., D. Dentoni, G. Meszoely, and S. Waddell. 2015. "The Complexity of Wicked Problems in Large System Change." *Journal of Organizational Change Management* 28, no. 6, pp. 993–1012, and Waddell, S., S. Waddock, S. Cornell, D. Dentoni, M. McLachlan, and G. Meszoely. 2014. "Large Systems Change." *Journal of Corporate Citizenship* 53, 5–30.

[25]   Ackoff, R.L., and J. Gharajedaghi. 1996. "Reflections on Systems and their Models." *Systems Research 13*, no. 1, pp. 13–23.

[26]   Koestler, A. 1968. *The Ghost in the Machine.* New York, NY: Random House.

[27]   Koestler, *The Ghost in the Machine.*

other holons that are nested within them. For example, the circulatory system in a human body is a holon—it is both something distinct and whole itself and an integrated part of the larger entity—the body. Socio-economic systems are also comprised of holons—for example, businesses comprise industries, yet are distinct (systemic) entities in and of themselves, and industries themselves make up the larger complex of societies.

A nation, for example, is a complex system comprised of different states or provinces, many ecological systems, villages, towns, and cities, and many different types of institutions, including communities and families and, ultimately, individuals. At each level these subsystems can be viewed as whole in themselves and also as integral parts of the larger systems of which they are a part. Similarly, even nations are often part of regional blocks like the European Union, which themselves are part of a global planetary system. We could take this further since human societies are themselves part of and bound to nature or the earth's ecosystems, which are part of the planetary system of our sun, which is part of the Milky Way, and, well, you get the picture.

Such systems need to be understood and dealt with holistically, but they are comprised of numerous other "whole" systems, for example, towns or cities, that also can be considered to be wholes comprised of multiple interactive parts, many of which are themselves "wholes," nested within or interactive with each other. Living systems tend to be what complexity scientists call self-organizing, often becoming ever-more complex and diverse when they are successfully developing, and sometimes operating at what complexity scientists call the "edge of chaos," meaning that they can "tip" suddenly in to a wholly new state (including collapse).

Wickedness

In addition to being complex adaptive systems, human institutions and societies are also fraught with wicked problems. The term "wicked" is used to describe a type of problem that is unbounded, poorly formulated and structured, with no clear beginnings or endings, with multiple stakeholders of different points of view about problem definition, solutions, and means of possible resolution. Such problems tend to be unique with no real solutions feasible and no way of actually determining when they are resolved, or to necessarily satisfy all of the problem's relevant stake-holders with a given approach or "solution."[28]

Complex systems, particularly socioecological systems, are filled with wicked problems, and, as must be clear, both complexity and wicked-ness share important characteristics that are relevant to system change. These characteristics include lack of problem definition, needing to be approached holistically (as well as in their parts, sometimes), dynamism and nonlinearity, with emergent and coevolutionary processes without clear resolutions or outcomes able to be specified, and with little pre-dictability. In both, relationships can create recognizable patterns, but there is no ability to predict (or "plan") for specific outcomes, because of the interactions, dynamics, and connectedness of different elements of the system. Each system and each problem within a system is uniquely based in its context, and initiatives to change the system cannot be com-pletely "withdrawn" or stopped once they have been started because the very starting of them will have already changed system dynamics and relationships.[29]

Complexity and Wickedness Together

Complexity and wickedness have similar characteristics that make "plan-ning" transformative change next to impossible. That is why having a guiding narrative (framework, set of memes, story, and/or articulated purposes) is so important. The overarching narrative has the potential to provide a kind of glue that holds varied aspects of a system together and guides them towards similar ends and aspirations. Issues and problems in such contexts, that is, virtually all social and ecological contexts, are

---

[28] See Waddock et al., Complexity. Sources for wicked problems include Rittel, H.W., and M.M. Webber. 1973. "Dilemmas in a General Theory of Planning." *Policy Sciences* 4, no. 2, pp. 155–69, who first elaborated the concept of wicked problems, and Churchman, C.W. 1967. "Guest Editorial: Wicked Problems." *Management Science* 14, no. 4, B141–42, who gave the construct its name.

[29] Waddock et al., Complexity, for further elaboration and justification of these ideas.

open-ended, with no clear beginnings or endings.[30] They have permeable boundaries, which means that they overlap with each other in ways that make teasing them apart nearly impossible. Issues and problems tend to be poorly formulated and ill-structured, and dynamically interactive.

Typically, there are numerous stakeholders in socioecological systems in different types of organizations and communities, at different levels, who have varying perspectives on the nature, causes, and best resolutions of the issues and problems. Healthy complex systems, like healthy ecosystems and social systems, are self-organizing and adaptive to changes. They have a tendency to become more complex, avoiding what chaos theorists call the "edge of chaos," a place where systemic collapse or at least dramatic state change occurs. Such "edges" were experienced with the Global Financial Crisis of 2007–2008 and the 2020 Covid-19 pandemic. Change in these types of systems is emergent and nonlinear, rather than straightforward, since interacting elements make specific shifts quite unpredictable.

All of these characteristics, including the dynamic interconnectedness of both stakeholders and issues, make predicting outcomes, planning changes, and directing actions around transformative system change difficult at best. What the nature of these systems mean for transformative (or any systemic) change is that it cannot be "directed" from the top, and, indeed, can begin just about anywhere in the system where a stakeholder starts to initiative a change and gains leverage. Further, because of the interconnectivity and dynamism, ripple effects from any initiatives are likely to spread out through the system in unpredictable—and unstoppable—ways. These characteristics highlight the need for a powerful

---

[30]   The classic formulation of wicked problems comes from Rittel and Webber, Dilemmas in a general theory of planning, and Churchman, Wicked problems. Classic insights into complexity and complex adaptive systems are given by Kauffman, S. 1995. *At Home in the Universe: The Search for the Laws of Self-Organization and Complexity*. NY: Oxford University Press, Capra, F. 2005. "Complexity and Life." *Theory, Culture and Society* 22, no. 5, pp. 33–44; Capra, F., and P.L. Luisi. 2014. *The Systems View of Life: A Unifying Vision*. Cambridge, UK: Cambridge University Press; and Grégoire, N., and I. Prigogine. 1989. *Exploring Complexity: An Introduction*. New York: W.H. Freeman and Company, among others. Ideas here are derived from these scientists as synthesized in Waddock et al., Complexity, cited above.

and resonant set of memes and related stories or narratives to help guide the various actors likely to initiate changes and provide a framework for actions that tend in the same direction.

Societies and Complexly Wicked Systems

Societies—socioeconomic and socioecological systems are large, complex adaptive systems, to use complexity theory language—are ones that have breadth, depth, and scale with multiple embedded subsystems.[31,32] Breadth means that these systems are typically comprised of numerous different types of entities with a range of functions and roles.[33] Well-functioning human systems are comprised of many different types of organizations and institutions that constitute communities and societies, creating variety and diversity of roles and functioning. So, for example, in societies there are businesses, nonprofit or nongovernmental organizations, governmental organizations, schools, hospitals, and a whole array of other civil society institutions that collectively constitute the society, while being "wholes" in themselves simultaneously.

Societies as whole systems are comprised of different sectors, typically thought of as the public or governmental sector, the business or economic sector, and the civil society sector, in which many institutions perform varying functions and that interact in many ways. Similarly, in healthy ecosystems, many different types of entities have different roles in the system. For instance, a healthy forest will have multiple types of trees and other plants, animals of a variety of sizes and species, and all sorts of other biota that literally form a community and nurture each other, often in unrecognized ways.[34] Is not that kind of supportive community exactly what we wish for our communities, nations, and ultimately the

---

[31] Waddell, S., S. Waddock, S. Cornell, D. Dentoni, M. McLachlan, and G. Meszoely. 2014. "Large Systems Change." *Journal of Corporate Citizenship* 53, pp. 5–30.

[32] Waddell, S. 2016. *Change for the Audacious: A Doer's Guide to Large Systems Change for Flourishing Futures*. Boston: Networking Action.

[33] Here see Waddell, *Change for the Audacious*.

[34] Wohlleben, P. 2016. *The Hidden Life of Trees: What They Feel, How They Communicate Discoveries from a Secret World*. Vancouver: Greystone Books.

whole world? We will speak more about healthy ecosystems later when we talk about what gives life to flourishing systems. In sum: numerous different types, sizes, and species in what Petra Kuenkel and I called "requisite diversity"[35] populate healthy systems and have different roles and functions to give the system its breadth.

Depth in large systems means that multiple levels coexist simultaneously, inextricably linked with each other. Many of these levels are "holons,"[36] wholes within wholes that are part of larger wholes. For example, in human societies, there is the family, which exists within the local community, which exists within the province or state, up to the region, the nation, and ultimately the whole world, each of which constitutes its own level and is inextricably connected to the others levels as well. Another way of phrasing depth is to think about local to global dimensions, for example, cities, states or provinces, regions (like New England in the United States), and nation states. Natural ecosystems also have depth, for example individual entities like bacteria live in animals, plants, trees, which live in complexes like forests, plains, or oceans, which themselves exist within the context of bigger land masses or the planet itself.

Beyond breadth and depth, and vitally important to this analysis, large systems have scale, that is, they are big, with issues and problems that have characteristics of both complexity and wickedness. These wickedly complex systems[37] mean that each issue or problem is as a symptom of other problems in the system. Issues are tangled up with each other and cannot really be separated if they are to remain recognizable. For example, climate change, poverty, terrorism, or inequality, are representative of wicked problems and they take place in the context of societies and communities that are themselves complex adaptive systems, in the bigger

---

[35] Waddock, S., and P. Kuenkel. May 2019. "What Gives Life to Large System Change?" *Organization and the Natural Environment* doi: https://journals.sagepub.com/doi/10.1177/1086026619842482

[36] Koestler, *The Ghost in the Machine.*

[37] Ideas about wicked problems are drawn from Rittel, H.W., and M.M. Webber. 1973. "Dilemmas in a General Theory of Planning." *Policy Sciences 4*, no. 2, pp. 155–69, and Churchman, C.W. 1967. "Guest Editorial: Wicked Problems." *Management Science* 14, no. 4, B141–B42.

context of ecological systems, which are also complex systems.[38] Indeed, the issue of climate change has been termed a "super-wicked problem"[39] because of its many complexities, facets, stakeholders, implications, and "wicked" issues.

All of these characteristics mean that there are no definitive resolutions that are likely to fully satisfy the multiplicity of stakeholders to a given issue or problem. Indeed, stakeholders are likely to have different ideas about the nature and definition of the problem and the best means of solving it; they likely also differ in what they think a good solution might be. Further, figuring out where the endpoint that "solves" the problem is not necessarily feasible either, as when one issue looks resolved, others are likely to be generated. Predictability is also an issue, although patterns can emerge that can provide insights when they are mapped and understood. In addition, because of as path dependency, once an initiative or solution is attempted, there is no way to go back to the original state because the interactive effects of any action mean that the system itself has changed.

Thinking about transformative system change through the two lenses of complexity and wickedness helps explain why such transformation is so difficult. In systems with all of these dynamics and interactions, change cannot be "planned" in any orderly or logical way, despite that many might like to think that is possible. In such systems, there are many factors that will likely result in change—technological advances and changes, public opinion, legislative, regulatory, and policy shifts, media attention, leadership, and, of course, deliberate change strategies and innovations.

---

[38]   Some insight into complexity and chaos theories, which contribute to this way of perceiving systems include: Kauffman, *At Home in the Universe*; Nicolis and Prigogine, *Exploring Complexity*; Ilya Prigogine, and Isabelle Stengers, *Order Out of Chaos: Man's New Dialogue with Nature*. Boulder, CO: New Science Library; Stacey, R.D. 1984. "The Science of Complexity: An Alternative Perspective for Strategic Change Processes." *Strategic Management Journal* 16, no. 6, pp. 477–95; Capra, F. 2005. "Complexity and Life." *Theory, Culture and Society* 22, no. 5, pp. 33–44; Capra, F. 1995. *The Web of Life*. New York: Doubleday; and Capra and Luisi. *The Systems View of Life*. Among many others.
[39]   Levin, K., B. Cashore, S. Bernstein, and G. Auld. 2012. "Overcoming the Tragedy of Super Wicked Problems: Constraining our Future Selves to Ameliorate Global Climate Change." *Policy Sciences* 45, no. 2, pp. 123–52.

System changes typically take place under the aegis of some sort of story or narrative, complete with a supporting set of memes that allow different actors to tell different stories as relevant to their circumstances. The story that we tell ourselves is a vital part of transcending the current mindset, and changing the way people think about our world—the mindsets that we carry in our heads every day that affect how we are in the world. In fact, I believe that it is the story or narrative that is the core way that the type of purposeful system change now needed can be guided.[40] In the next chapter, we explore the relevance and importance of stories, narratives, and memes in bringing about large system change.

---

[40] Waddock, S. 2020. "Thinking Transformational Systems Change." *Journal of Change Management,* online first doi: https://doi.org/10.1080/14697017.2020.1 737179

CHAPTER 4

Stories, Narratives, and Memes: Foundations of Cultural Mythologies

The last chapter discussed a bit about how complexity and wickedness—wicked complexity or complex wickedness—characterize socioeconomic systems. I noted that achieving purposeful system change in such systems is difficult at best because of these characteristics. That said, one way in which systems do change is when the stories or narratives that describe what it means to be in that system also change. Changing the narrative allows people to change their mindset, perspective, or paradigm—how they frame and understanding the world, which in turn allows them to change attitudes, behaviors, and operating practices. This chapter focuses on the fundamentals of the power of stories, narratives, and memes in system transformation.

The Tale of Neoliberalism

Humans are storytelling animals. We tell stories to make sense of the world and to entertain us. We tell and invent stories to share wisdom and advance learning. The neoliberal narrative has become a prevailing force that shapes not only the economy but also the whole societies in which economies exist. Ironically, neoliberalism denies that societies even exist (or as former UK Prime Minister Margaret Thatcher once said, "There is no such thing as society"). It ignores the natural environment as well. In the dominance of this way of thinking, there is little recognition of the fact that societies breed economies—not vice versa. From the nested systems perspective discussed in the last chapter, in fact, societies are the bigger entity and nested within them are economies, for economic activity is only part of what societies encompass. They also educate, care for, govern, and do many other things for the people (and other living beings) within them.

Perhaps even more fundamentally, in neoliberalism there is no attention to the reality that societies themselves, as well as us human beings, are products of, dependent on, and intimately connected to nature. Neoliberal thinking thus ignores the impacts of industrial production, economic activity, and human population growth on the natural environment. It views such impacts as externalities, which in economic thinking are (positive or negative) side-effects of production and other commercial (or other) activities. Positive externalities benefit societies and other living beings from the development of, say, parks or preserved wetlands by producing what are known as public goods. Negative externalities, or public "bads," are costs that are dumped onto societies by production and other processes, for which the originators of the costs do not pay. From a systems perspective, someone has to pay—and it can be the health of the system or its participants that suffer. The costs are somewhere in the system and for many externalities we all pay in some way. That such externalities can be produced without consequences to the businesses that produce them is one implication of neoliberal thinking.

Another implication, which comes from the idea that humans have the right to dominate nature, explored earlier, is that there are perceived to be endless raw materials available for exploitation by human beings. Further, humans have every right to do that exploitation, again without regard to the consequences of doing so. Thus, there is little regard for consequences of that exploitation on other living beings or even on human societies, and a strong belief that endless economic growth is not only feasible but also desirable. Even the popular term "sustainable development," which originated in the 1987 Brundtland Commission Report called *Our Common Future*,[1] implies that continuous development can in fact be sustainable. But as John Ehrenfeld and Andrew Hoffman point out in their book *Flourishing*, there is a huge difference between actually living

---

[1] Brundtland, G.H. 1987. *Our Common Future: World Commission on Environmental Development.* Oxford, UK: Oxford University Press, Oxford, UK.

within earth's parameters or being truly sustainable and simply being "less unsustainable,"[2] which is what most of today's enterprises aim for.

Activist and writer George Monbiot captures the problem neatly in an interview published in *Truthout*:

> Neoliberalism is, at heart, a self-serving racket: an elaborate theory that serves as an excuse for the very rich to release themselves from the constraints of democracy: tax, regulation, decent pay and conditions for their workers, care for the living world and all the other decencies we owe to each other. But the reason it caught on is that it was framed within the classic political narrative structure, that has worked again and again throughout history, that I call the Restoration Story. This goes as follows:
>
> Disorder afflicts the land, caused by powerful and nefarious forces working against the interests of humanity. The hero—who might be one person or a group of people—revolts against this disorder, fights the nefarious forces, overcomes them despite great odds and restores order.[3]

The story that Monbiot points to is representative of the classic "hero's journey," as told by the great mythologist Joseph Campbell.[4] Campbell describes this core story as a monomyth because of its ubiquity globally in different cultures and contexts. Campbell describes the hero's journey as follows:

---

[2] Ehrenfeld, J., and A. Hoffman. 2013. *Flourishing: A Frank Conversation about Sustainability*. Palo Alto: Stanford University Press.

[3] Karlin, M. 2017. "George Monbiot: We Need a New Political Story of Empathy and Sharing to Replace Neoliberalism." Truthout Interview. October 22, 2017, http://truth-out.org/opinion/item/42340-george-monbiot-we-need-a-new-political-story-of-empathy-and-sharing-to-replace-neoliberalism; also published on George Monbiot's website, http://monbiot.com/2017/11/02/becoming-unstoppable/

[4] Campbell, J. 2008. *The Hero with a Thousand Faces*, Vol. 17. Novato, CA: New World Library.

A hero ventures forth from the world of common day into a region of supernatural wonder: fabulous forces are there encountered and a decisive victory is won: the hero comes back from this mysterious adventure with the power to bestow boons on his fellow man.[5]

This story has universal qualities that can be tapped to build a convincing and effective new story—or, more accurately, to develop a relevant set of memes that can be used to construct multiple, locally relevant narratives and stories. Christopher Vogler[6] has synthesized this hero's journey, which is similar to the processes that shamans as healers undergo as they assume their healing powers.[7] In the process that Vogler and Campbell describe, the hero (or healer) is called to adventure because of some issue or problem. Often with the guidance of mentors or sages, the hero sets off on the journey, crossing some threshold into a new world. In the new context, mentors, sages, and allies help the hero who is passing through obstacles, ordeals, and various tests. Finally, after numerous tests and trials, the hero reaches the abyss, low point, or crisis, where a sort of death to the old ways and transformational rebirth takes place. There the hero is given a boon or gift to take back to the normal world, while making whatever atonement for the past is needed. In reentering the familiar world, the hero is, in a sense, resurrected, and able to bring the boon or gift back to those who need it.

Earlier, we explored the powerful narrative developed and promulgated for many years by neoliberals, which today shapes much thinking about the nature, functions, and purposes of the economy and its major institutions, businesses. When we look at this monomyth's broad outlines, we can see that in its essence it was the story that neoliberals told in their quest to "save" the world, and particularly business from the ravages

---

[5]   Campbell, J. 2008. *The Hero with a Thousand Faces*, p. 23.

[6]   Vogler, C. 1985. "A Practical Guide to Joseph Campbell's the Hero with a Thousand Faces." *Hero's Journey*, URL: http://thinking-differently.com/creativity/wp-content/uploads/2014/01/The-Heros-Journey.pdf

[7]   Waddock, S. 2017. *Healing the World: Today's Shamans as Difference Makers*. London: Greenleaf/Routledge.

of constraints against "free" enterprise, as Monbiot outlines.[8] A major step in accomplishing transformative system towards flourishing for all is to reframe the story we tell ourselves about the world (societies and economies), and, particularly about humans' relationships to each other and to nature.

Using elements of the hero's journey and stepping into the belief systems and ideologies of people in the systems that need to change may provide helpful understanding how to construct stories that work. To be successful, new stories probably need to somehow take the shape of the hero's journey, identifying the problem and the "heroes" (perhaps multiple or collective) who can counter the problem, fighting the dark and mysterious forces that create obstacles along the way, much as the framers of the neoliberal thought did with their story. It is clear from the impacts that the neoliberal narrative has had just how important the story we tell ourselves is. It is exactly this sentiment that activist and global thought leader David Korten has captured in the title of his book, *Change the Story, Change the Future*.[9] That is what we are attempting to do in developing a story that poses a broader, more complete, and arguably considerably more realistic alternative to neoliberalism's core assumptions.

In ancient times, and today in Indigenous cultures, people recognized that stories are vitally important to their well-being. Stories about who we are as a people, how we relate to each other, what our origins are, and how we fit into nature frame what anthropologists call cultural mythology. They are grounded in what are known as origin stories, which shape belief systems about how the world operates and what the community's relationship to the world is. Many shamans, medicine men or women, in Indigenous cultures believe that when their patients get sick, it is because there is something wrong with the cultural mythology in which the community believes.[10] To heal the patient in such circumstances, the healer or

---

[8] George Monbiot: We Need a New Political Story.
[9] Korten, D.C. 2015. *Change the Story, Change the Future: A Living Economy for a Living Earth*. San Francisco: Berrett-Koehler Publishers.
[10] Ideas about shamanism and cultural mythology are from: James, D. 1986. "Universal Aspects of Symbolic Healing: A Theoretical Synthesis." *American Anthropologist* 88, no. 1, pp. 56–69.

shaman needs to reshape the mythology. That is, they need, as we do now, to tell a new story that is more in keeping with reality and that allows for healing whatever issues are facing the system.

Today many observers can witness the consequences of the neoliberal story. We see its impacts in climate change, growing inequality, increased political divisiveness, the pandemic, over-exploitation of natural resources, harmful farming and industrial practices, and too many other ills fostered in the name of growth and efficiency to name. We see the power of the neoliberal story when we recognize the dominance of the economic story, with its economic orientation, values, and beliefs. That story now overpowers other possible stories about humans living in balance or harmony with nature and in civil community with each other, including spiritual values, connection to other people and other living beings, stewardship, or a raft of other possibilities. It is in the nightly news and the political divisions that are driving people apart in so many places.

It is long past time to shift that story towards societies that foster connectedness or relationship and life rather than simply wealth as measured by finances and material goods. Stories and narratives and, we will demonstrate below, especially the memes or core units of culture like words, phrases, images, and symbols, out of which stories and narratives are constructed, are powerful vehicles for creating social stability as well as social change. Creating resonant, believable, and coherent new stories is a first and very important step towards the large system change needed today. Only with such stories can the world's populace bring about flourishing, dignity for all, and well-being, memes that we believe need to be important elements of the new story. That is because the stories that we tell ourselves shape how we react to events in the world, what our beliefs and attitudes are, and what kinds of organizations and institutions we are willing and able to support.

The Power of Narratives, Stories, and Memes

Stories and narratives have multiple purposes in human societies and cultures. They can, for example, frame the community's origin mythologies and culture, and shape ideas about what our place in the world is. In a very real way, stories and narratives help provide a sense of identity, purpose, and place when we can relate to them. Stories and narratives, particularly with the memes or core units of culture that underpin them, also are influential ways of communicating points of view, shaping belief systems, engaging with others, and sometimes implicitly, enhancing understanding of relationships that exist within a given setting.[11]

In the context of systemic change, dominant or prominent stories and narratives can provide an overview or, in a sense, a vision, of hopes, dreams, and ambitions. In that sense, new stories when resonant, effective, and constructive can provide an inspirational and aspirational sense of the future that opens pathways for change and transformation.[12] As the hero's journey metanarrative or monomyth suggests, stories with the right elements can, in a sense, hook us into their perspective, especially when they draw on deep existing cultural norms and beliefs as the neoliberal narrative did.

Familiar stories have a common set of elements—a storyteller or narrator, characters and a protagonist, a plot (often based on some version of the hero's journey) that provides energy that moves the story along, a context that has physical and time dimensions, some sort of recognizable shape or form, and enough truth that there is appeal to the narrative.[13] Stories and narratives—here we use these terms interchangeably—in the public and policy contexts have four key elements: (i) they provide a setting or context in which we can see relevant issues or problems; (ii) they have characters who typically act as victims, villains, or heroes; (iii) some stories have a "moral" that provides solutions to the identified problem; and (iv) the plot or storyline links all of the other elements together.[14] At the national level, stories can take the form of national ideologies[15] that

---

[11] Moezzi, M., K.B. Janda, and S. Rotmann. 2017. "Using Stories, Narratives, and Storytelling in Energy and Climate Change Research." *Energy Research and Social Science* 31, pp. 1–10.

[12] Moezzi, Janda, and Rotmann.

[13] Lazarevic, D., and H. Valve. 2017. "Narrating Expectations for the Circular Economy: Towards a Common and Contested European Transition." *Energy Research and Social Science* 31, 60–69.

[14] Lazarevic and Valve, 60.

[15] Lodge, G. C., and E.F. Vogel, eds. 1987. *Ideology and National Competitiveness: An Analysis of Nine Countries.* Cambridge, MA: Harvard Business Press.

characterize the nature, origins, and culture of the country and frame how citizens see the world, albeit this "story" comes through with many voices, whose ideas sometimes conflict and sometimes agree, and without particular clarity.[16]

Narratives and stories powerfully convey identity, values, and attributes of a given character in the story, whether that is a person, mythological figure, nation, or even an abstract concept like the economy, in the case of the neoliberal narrative. In doing so, dominant and popular narratives and stories create the cultural mythology that lies at the core of human societies[17] and culture. They generate core beliefs about those societies, ultimately shaping attitudes and behaviors that result from those beliefs.[18]

Local myths or stories enhance understanding of organizations, communities, and whole nations,[19] which in turn helps characterize their uniqueness, and provides a specific context that allows for place-based identity. Indeed, Indigenous peoples often identify closely with their land of origin, their literal place in the world, which makes knowing their origin stories and mythologies particularly important.[20] The neoliberal narrative is, in a sense, a one-size-fits-all story, because it takes the values derived from Enlightenment thinking and assumes that this framing of economies will fit every situation, culture, and place. In reality, every

---

[16]   Malone, E., N.E. Hultman, K.L. Anderson, and V. Romeiro. 2017. "Stories about Ourselves: How National Narratives Influence the Diffusion of Large-Scale Energy Technologies." *Energy Research and Social Science* 31, pp. 70–76.

[17]   McNeill, W.H. 1982. "The Care and Repair of Public Myth." *Foreign Affairs* 61, no. 1, pp. 1–13.

[18]   McNeil, "The care and Repair of Public Myth," Suggests that Such Beliefs are 'Based on Faith more than Fact' (p. 1).

[19]   See, for example, Meyer, J.W., and B. Rowan. 1977. "Institutionalized Organizations: Formal Structure as Myth and Ceremony." *American Journal of Sociology* 83, no. 2, pp. 340–63; and Dow, J. 1986. "Universal Aspects of Symbolic Healing: A Theoretical Synthesis." *American Anthropologist* 88, no. 1, pp. 56–69.

[20]   Martinez, D. 2010. "The Value of Indigenous Ways of Knowing to Western Science and Environmental Sustainability." *Journal of Sustainability Education* http://www.susted.com/wordpress/content/the-value-of-indigenous-ways-of-knowing-to-western-science-and-environmental-sustainability_2010_05/

nation and community is unique. Since people living in the developed Western world have different world views than do Indigenous peoples or people in the global South and East, it is important that stories and narratives can be adapted to/develop from their particular context. Given this reality, it is highly unlikely that any single story will serve everyone. That is where memes come in.

Memes: The Building Blocks of Stories and Narratives

Considerable research indicates that the language we speak shapes how we perceive and act in the world.[21] Language consists of words and phrases constitute the stories and narratives that shape thinking. These words and phrases are memes, and they are an often-overlooked element of understanding how the narratives and stories that shape societies are constructed, and, ultimately, of large system change.[22] We all know about Internet memes at some level, but many are unfamiliar with a more fundamental understanding of the term. The term "meme" was coined by biologist Richard Dawkins, who was searching for a cultural equivalent to the idea of the gene, or sequences of DNA or RNA, the foundation of heritable traits.[23] Memes, short for mimemes, are ideas, behaviors, or styles that spread from one individual to others, mostly intact, just as genes are passed along from one generation to the next.

A meme is the core unit of culture, according to Susan Blackmore, who has extensively studied memes. Memes are ubiquitous, surrounding us, and can be just about any idea that replicates more or less intact from one individual mind to another; things like words, phrases, images, symbols, artistic expressions.[24] Think about the Wall Street Bull, and more recently Fearless Girl statues, for example, or any iconic image. Such

---

[21] Boroditsky, L. 2011. "How Language Shapes Thought." *Scientific American* 304, no. 2, pp. 62–65.

[22] This section draws from Waddock, S. 2015. "Reflections: Intellectual Shamans, Sensemaking, and Memes in Large System Change." *Journal of Change Management* 15, no. 4, pp. 259–73.

[23] Dawkins, R. 2006. *The Selfish Gene*. London: Oxford University Press.

[24] Blackmore, S. *The Meme Machine: The Power of the Meme.*

images, which replicate widely, provide symbolic meanings also shared among relevant populations. Memes coalesce in stories or what Blackmore calls "memeplexes." Memplexes are collections of memes that gel, as in a story or narrative, to convey an idea, vision, story, or other message, and sometimes to create important cultural mythologies.

Successful memes resonate with their recipients; otherwise they would not pass from one individual to the next. In thinking about system transformation, it is important to consider what are the memes that underpin the new story to be conveyed—or the narratives that are constructed? Different cultural, national, ethnic, and other contexts generate different memes, which accounts in many ways for their differences. At the same time, shared memes create common understandings, shape values, norms, ideologies, and belief systems, as well as attitudes, and, ultimately, behaviors and practices.

The Coca-Cola symbol, for example, is widely recognized all over the world and is known to symbolize the soft drink. Similarly, the Apple logo—an apple with a bite taken from it—is globally resonant and helps the company send messages about the nature and quality of its products. The idea of marriage equality for same-sex couples became a resonant meme in the United States (and elsewhere around the world), replacing earlier memes like gay pride or gay rights, and causing significant shifts in public attitudes that ultimately resulted in the U.S. Supreme Court legalizing same-sex marriage.[25] Resonant memes are thus central to system transformation, because different people can use them in different ways in different contexts, thus providing the essentials of a common story or set of understandings—but that are place-, culturally, or societally appropriate. But this approach works only if there is agreement about these shared memes.

Memes are important to how people frame worldviews, as well how they relate to and interact with others. They help generate what linguist George Lakoff calls frames that provide understanding and coherence

---

[25] Waddock, S., and S. Waddell. 2018. "The Transformational Change Challenge of Memes: The Case of Marriage Equality." *Business and Society*, published online first, Doi: https://doi.org/10.1177/0007650318816440 (accessed December 2018).

in systems.[26] Memes and the stories constructed of them can illuminate whether change is even possible, and what types of ideas, goals, and futures might be possible. Memes can block or shape possibilities, create obstacles to change or opportunities for change. Memes are ideas that are memorable—that is why they replicate and have "staying power."[27] Yet to date memes are little understood in transformational change processes.

Think, for example, about the words and phrases (that is, memes) that underlie the neoliberal narrative: maximizing wealth, free markets, free trade, individual responsibility and freedom, private property, endless growth, less government, and efficiency. All of these, which constitute how neoliberalism is framed, are memes that resonate broadly, particularly in the American psyche, with its national ideology of individualism, pioneering spirit, personal responsibility, and "can do" optimism. These memes, however, downplay shared life, community, relationships, and flourishing for all (not just humans) in the ultimate interest of gains for the elite. They ignore shared responsibilities, fairness, community, and collective well-being, as well as ideas like connection, mutual responsibilities, and the importance of relationships. Nowhere in the neoliberal agenda is there mention of reverence for each other, for nature and her many beings, or any sense of spirit. Even dignity, and well-being for all, elements that we believe need to be at the core of new narratives, are not part of the neoliberal agenda.

Dominant or popular narratives and stories are comprised of a coherent set of memes and can be influential levers for change in large systems, particularly because successful memes "infect" minds as viruses do.[28] They provide overall guidance about what types of initiatives make sense in the context of given story or narrative. Stories, narratives, and their underlying memes powerfully shape attitudes, ideas, thinking, and

---

[26] Lakoff, G. 2014. *The All New Don't Think of an Elephant! Know Your Values and Frame the Debate.* White River Junction, VT: Chelsea Green Publishing.

[27] Gleick, J. 2011. "What Defines a Meme?" *Smithsonian Magazine* http://cosmicscribbler.com/erau/What_Defines_a_Meme.pdf, p. 3.

[28] Williams, R. 2004. "Management Fashions and Fads: Understanding the Role of Consultants and Managers in the Evolution of Ideas." *Management Decision* 42, no. 6, pp. 769–780.

ultimately behaviors and practices, both individually and organization-
ally, in important ways.[29]

Mindsets and Memes Matter

Changing mindsets and, more importantly as Donella Meadows noted in
her important discussion of "Leverage Points: Places to Intervene in a System,"[30] transcending the paradigms that form mindsets,[31] is fundamental
to thinking about how to transform today's fossil-fuel, finance-oriented,
inequitable system towards something more aligned with the constraints
and capacities nature affords. To the extent that many people are "stuck"
in the neoliberal mindset, it becomes hard to shift towards a different way
of being and acting in the world. That is because it seems that there is a
sort of "fixed" orientation to the system that exists, a sense that "this is
how it always was" or that there is only one way to organize the world and
that is through markets.

Mindset shift, and the ability to transcend paradigms (mindsets),
according to Meadows, are the most powerful change levers. Very much a
human- (as opposed to Earth- or nature-) centric, the neoliberal mindset
theoretically relies on the "science" of economics. Its core ideas of wealth
maximization for a single set of stakeholders, that is, the shareholders,
and individual liberty at the expense of collective good (which is believed
to be nonexistent) are set in a context in which markets will resolve all
social and ecological problems though continual growth. Much evidence,
as noted earlier, suggests these assumptions are problematic at best.

---

[29] See, for example, Blackmore, S. 2013. *The Meme Machine and the Power of
Memes*; Janda, K.B., and M. Topouzi. 2013. "Closing the Loop: Using Hero
Stories and Learning Stories to Remake Energy Policy." Proceedings of ECEEE
Summer Study, European Council for an Energy-Efficient Economy, *Presqu'île
de Giens, France*; and Janda, K.B., and M. Topouzi. 2015. "Telling Tales: Using
Stories to Remake Energy Policy." *Building Research and Information* 43, no. 4,
pp. 516–33.
[30] Meadows, D. 1999. *Leverage Points: Places to Intervene in a System*. Harland,
VT: The Sustainability Institute. URL: http://donellameadows.org/archives/
leverage-points-places-to-intervene-in-a-system/
[31] Meadows, D. Leverage Points.

Yet humans do have the capacity for reflection, including reflection on self and on their impacts on the world around them. From a systems perspective, they can view the impacts and consequences of decisions made, and when there are problematic consequences (hopefully) see a path towards different decisions with different consequences. Indeed, management theorist Russell Ackoff once defined wisdom as the capacity to see the consequences of one's actions.[32] Wisdom is certainly needed to shift today's dominant mindset to one that engages broader dimensions of what it really means to be human in the best sense of that phrase.

Climate scientist Will Steffen and colleagues in calling for planetary stewardship seem to believe that such a mindset shift may be possible. Recognizing the importance of understanding human impacts on the world, while also acknowledging our reflective capabilities, this group notes:

> We are the first generation with the knowledge of how our activities influence the Earth System, and thus the first generation with the power and the responsibility to change our relationship with the planet.[33]

That new reality means that many more of us need to begin to take responsibility for the whole system—for rebalancing what is now greatly out of balance.

Further bolstering the importance of memes and mindsets, pragmatist philosopher and psychologist William James once noted, "Our beliefs are really rules for action."[34] That is, the mental models or mindsets that develop from our beliefs express how we see the world and in many ways shape how we act in the world as a result of those beliefs. Worldviews and mindsets shape the social realities or context in which humans live because what attended to, and where attention is placed in a sense becomes reality.

---

[32] Ackoff, R. 1975. *Redesigning the Future*. New York: Wiley.

[33] Steffen, Will., Å. Persson, L. Deutsch, J. Zalasiewicz, M. Williams, K. Richardson, C. Crumley, et al. 2011. "The Anthropocene: From Global Change to Planetary Stewardship." *Ambio* 40, no. 7, pp. 739–49.

[34] James, W. 1975. *Pragmatism*, Vol. 1, p. 24. Boston: Harvard University Press.

Whatever ideas in the mental model are enacted or put into practice then becomes the reality reflected in the emergent processes of (re-)developing mental models on an ongoing basis.[35]

Mindsets are established sets of attitudes or belief systems that frame a person's, a group's, or even an organization's perspective, worldview, or philosophy and influence how they live and act in the world. Mindsets can also determine how people view the future and the opportunities before them. Mindsets are formed by the narratives or stories that shape belief systems, and in particularly by the interpretation of the memes that underpin those stories. Neoliberalism's economic dominance means that other types of values are actually little taken into account. In many ways, this dominant narrative is so powerful, then, that it excludes other possible ways for framing humans' relationships to the world.

Extensive research on young students by psychologist Carol Dweck and her colleagues suggests that the students she studied tended to have either a fixed (about 40 percent of people) or growth mindset (also about 40 percent, with about 20 percent somewhere in the middle).[36] People with fixed mindsets believe that the talent you are born with is what you will have for life, that is, that "their basic abilities, their talents are just fixed traits." From that point of view, a person has only a certain amount of talent or intelligence, thus it is important to "look smart all the time and never look dumb," according to Dweck.[37] From the perspective of someone with a fixed mindset, a failure is a huge problem because it makes them look bad—and because they feel there is little they can do about it and that it somehow defines them.

---

[35]   Moosmayer, D.C., S. Waddock, L. Wang, M.P. Hühn, C. Dierksmeier, and C. Gohl. 2019. "Leaving the Road to Abilene: A Pragmatic Approach to Addressing the Normative Paradox of Responsible Management Education." *Journal of Business Ethics* 157, no. 4, 913–32, Doi: https://doi.org/10.1007/s10551-018-3961-8

[36]   Dweck, C.S. 2008. *Mindset: The New Psychology of Success.* New York, NY: Random House Digital, Inc., 2008; see also. Morehead, J. 2012. "Stanford University's Carol Dweck on the Growth Mindset and Education," OneDublin.org, URL: https://onedublin.org/2012/06/19/stanford-universitys-carol-dweck-on-the-growth-mindset-and-education/

[37]   Morehead, Stanford University's Carol Dweck.

A growth mindset, in contrast, fosters taking on challenges and learning from them, always striving to learn and do better. People with growth mindsets tend to persevere in the face of difficulties or mistakes, using the difficulties they are facing as motivators for working harder.[38] Adults seem to be able to take on numerous types of mindsets, including the one we have been discussing, the neoliberal economics mindset.

Other mindsets are possible. Research by Gary Klein and colleagues finds multiple mindsets in adults, including the fixed/growth dichotomy identified by Dweck, mindsets that are preoccupied with failure as opposed to an eagerness to discover, mindsets that evidence a desire to build trust, a willingness to cooperate, or an orientation to problem solving.[39] Further, Stephen Rhinesmith identified six "global mindsets": seeking context, viewing life as balancing contradictions, focusing on process, valuing diversity and emphasizing teamwork, seeing change as opportunity, and striving to be open to the unexpected.[40] Still others discuss what they term a sustainability mindset that helps people understand complex systems, enhancing self-awareness and spirituality, integrating across disciplines through systems thinking, and including the sustainability challenges discussed earlier.[41] Most mindsets, of course, are mixed to some extent, particularly for more growth-oriented individuals who may change their views, beliefs, and orientation over time.

Stuck in Neoliberalism?

In a sense, being "stuck" in the neoliberal narrative is a type of fixed mindset. It is an economic mindset that argues that there is one way to view the world, one set of values that matter, and one way for businesses and markets, and by extension whole societies (which are believed not to exist,

---

[38] Dweck, Mindset.

[39] Klein, G. 2016. "Mindsets: What they are and Why They Matter." *Psychology Today*, URL: https://psychologytoday.com/us/blog/seeing-what-others-dont/201605/mindsets

[40] Rhinesmith, S.H. 1992. "Global Mindsets for Global Managers." *Training and Development* 46, no. 10, pp. 63–69.

[41] Rimanoczy, I. 2017. *Big Bang Being: Developing the Sustainability Mindset.* London: Routledge.

making only economies real) to operate. From the perspective of neoliberalism, the only viable way to view the world is through the economically based lens of markets that are purportedly free, where self-interest matters most, and where as Margaret Thatcher famously stated, "There is no alternative," a meme that has been shortened to TINA.[42]

The "no alternative" belief means free markets, free trade, individual liberty, and constant growth, and the simultaneous sense that economy and financial wealth are what matter most in the world. In this same perspective, Margaret Thatcher also argued that "There is no such thing as society" in an interview with *Woman's Own* in 1987.[43] In that worldview or mindset, what matters most is financial wealth; wealth is the most important value. Despite what some believe, attaining wealth *is* a value—just not one that is particularly life-affirming.

Just how "stuck" in neoliberalism are mindsets and how easy might it be to shift the narrative to one that *is* more relational and life-affirming? Today there are many groups attempting to foster different ways of thinking particularly about economics and business. Such initiatives are framed as "new economics," and include, for example, The New Economics Foundation, Blue Economy, The New Economy Coalition; Living Economies, Evonomics, and Caring Economy, among many others.[44] Related initiatives are attempting to transform the nature of today's capitalism so that it takes stakeholders and the natural environment into better consideration, among them, Conscious Capitalism, Coalition for Inclusive Capitalism,

---

[42] Moncrieff, C. 2013. "Margaret Thatcher: In her Own Words." *Independent*, URL: https://independent.co.uk/news/uk/politics/margaret-thatcher-in-her-own-words-8564762.html

[43] Brian, D. (undated). Epitaph for the Eighties? "There is No Such thing as Society." http://briandeer.com/social/thatcher-society.htm

[44] For example, The New Economics Foundation, http://neweconomics.org/; Blue Economy, The New Economy Coalition, http://theblueeconomy.org/; Living Economies (http://livingeconomiesforum.org), Evonomics, (http://evonomics.com), Caring Economy (http://caringeconomy.org/). For a sense of just how many such alternative "new economy" entities exist, see the allies and members of WEAll, the Wellbeing Economy Alliance, www.wellbeingeconomy.org (accessed May 5, 2020).

Natural Capitalism Solutions, and Regenerative Capitalism.[45] Still others emphasize rethinking the system, among them, Volans: Breakthrough Capitalism, The Next System Project, and Ethical Markets.[46]

Even during the Covid-19 crisis, there are many calls are all to "return to business as usual," despite glaring evidence of the inequities and flaws in the system that the pandemic has revealed. The experience of the pandemic highlights the importance of pulling together messaging—memes—that support new ways for human beings to live in the world and engage with each other, as well other living and nonliving beings. It suggests, however, that such messaging, progressive in looking forward to a better future that embraces the well-being and dignity of all still needs considerable work if mindsets are to shift away from neoliberalism.

---

[45] Conscious Capitalism (http://consciouscapitalism.org/), Coalition for Inclusive Capitalism (http://inc-cap.com/), Natural Capitalism Solutions (http://natcapsolutions.org/), Regenerative Capitalism (http://capitalinstitute.org/).

[46] Volans: Breakthrough Capitalism (http://volans.com/), The Next System Project (http://thenextsystem.org/), and Ethical Markets (http://ethicalmarkets.com/).

CHAPTER 5

Accomplishing Transformational System Change

Chapter 4 explored the ways in which the current mindset—the most powerful change lever according to Donella Meadows—is "stuck" in the powerful messaging of neoliberalism. This chapter begins the exploration of how to move beyond that stuckness. Neoliberalism has manifested in the systems that are collapsing all around us. From the exigencies posed by the novel Coronavirus and other potential pandemics, to the impacts of long-term diminishment of the efficacy of governments, cracks are appearing. From short-term thinking and exploitive practices on the part of businesses, to abusive food and industrial agriculture practices, topsoil erosion, deforestation, and numerous other socioecological ills that have resulted in climate change, ecosystem collapses, and numerous sustainability crises, today's systems are fraught with crises.

It has long been one of my sayings that there is nothing like a good crisis to create change. If Covid-19 does nothing else—assuming enough of us survive—it highlights the potential for system change in a positive direction. It is important to recognize that change *will* already have taken place once the pandemic eases—it will have already taken place and it will be impossible to put that genie back into the bottle. Given the crisis and its aftermath, it is high time to think about changing this system—towards one that fosters flourishing for all.

If we really want to achieve flourishing for all—including all of nature's beings—then pretty much the whole of today's systems are subject to transformative change. That includes businesses, our governments and political systems, educational institutions, even churches, and civil society and NGO enterprises. Change potentially even includes the way we live in our families and communities and how we relate to other people.

Accomplishing purposeful and positive transformative change of that scale is certainly a daunting task. Yet if we are to meet the challenges posed by the threat of more pandemics, climate change, sociopolitical dissension and unrest, growing inequality, sustainability, terrorism, persistent poverty, a global jobs crisis, and the many other issues facing the world, nothing less is needed.

The thing is, with major disruptions from pandemics, climate change, sustainability issues, and socioeconomic unrest,[1] change will happen differently in different contexts and is unlikely to be centrally driven, given the nature of complexity and wickedness, as discussed earlier. Instead, there are several key aspects of transformative system change that need to be understood if we are to understand how to move transformation in purposefully guided directions. They are: (1) understanding core principles that "give life" to systems, (2) dealing effectively with the overarching (meta-)narrative (story) and accompanying memes that frame a new vision; and (3) understanding how change happens in complexly wicked contexts.

Emerging Stories and Narratives

As discussed in the last chapter, it is increasingly clear that there needs to be a compelling new story or narrative that guides actions and initiatives. Such a narrative helps people see what change is needed, understand why it will be better than the current situation, and enables them to move forward. Importantly, as part of developing the narrative, transformation agents need to articulate and shape the memes, or core images, phrases, and concepts that underlie the change because these memes are what affect attitudes, behaviors, and practices in a human system.[2] Further,

---

[1] Paul Gilding's book *The Great Disruption: How the Climate Crisis Will Transform the Global Economy*, Bloomsbury Publishing, 2011, outlines one such scenario. Gilding argues that massive innovation will then be developed by whoever and whatever systems remain intact or still able to innovate.

[2] Susan Blackmore, *The Meme Machine*.

many more people need to understand how the complex wickedness of the system and its problems affects what it is possible to change and how change happens. That understanding means accepting the reality that there will be many different types of changes likely taking place all at once, none of which can necessarily be planned in the traditional sense or even particularly well controlled, which makes the guidance of the narratives and their memes strikingly important.

Elsewhere and building on the seminal work of Meadows,[3] I outlined five core aspects of systems that can be "targeted" by transformation agents: purpose, perspectives, performance metrics, powers, and practices (including policies, procedures, processes, and practices).[4] This chapter and the next several will explore how some of these elements highlight what needs to change and provide insight into how that transformation might happen.

Perspectives

The last chapter explored the importance of memes, stories, and narratives in shaping paradigms, worldviews, and mindsets, and how deeply embedded neoliberalism is in the modern psyche. To change that requires lifting up and acknowledging very ancient Indigenous wisdom, along with newer perspectives about what gives "life" to systems to create an integrated worldview.

The reason why these insights—and the mindset to go with it—are important was recognized by Earth scientists in discussing the Anthropocene, that is, conditions on Earth influenced by human activities, is that:

The Anthropocene is a dynamic state of the Earth System, characterized by global environmental changes already significant enough to distinguish it from the Holocene, but with a momen-

---

[3] Donella Meadows, Leverage Points.

[4] Waddock, S. 2020. "Achieving Sustainability Requires Systemic Business Transformation." *Global Sustainability*, URL: https://doi.org/10.1017/sus2020.9. See also the working paper Waddock, S., and S. Waddell. 2020. *A 5Ps Framework for Purposeful System Transformation*. Boston College Working Paper.

tum that continues to move it away from the Holocene at a geologically rapid rate.[5]

New (or very ancient, depending on your point of view) understanding of humans' place on earth and associated mindsets represent the foundation needed to begin processes of systemic change towards a world of flourishing for all. As the idea of the Anthropocene indicates, however, human beings are *already* dramatically changing our earth's system. System transformation towards a flourishing, dignity, and well-being infused world, however, needs to be deliberately conceived if it is not to go awry. In this context, some scientists have called for what they term earth stewardship[6] or what others call earth system governance,[7] which emphasizes stewarding human systems as they interact with ecosystem stewardship.[8]

As discussed, transformational change is complex in the complexity science sense. Transformational system change inherently crosses multiple boundaries. These boundaries could be sectoral, industry, organizational, institutional, or, in the global context, national, regional, and state.[9] Many different people and initiatives, institutions, organizations, and enterprises are likely to be interested in any type of change efforts in a complex system. Further, these different people and institutions are likely to approach change from different perspectives, with different (sometimes competing) goals, and with multiple approaches, paradigms, and mindsets.

---

[5] Will Steffen et al. The Anthropocene.

[6] Chapin, F.S., M.E. Power, S.T.A. Pickett, A. Freitag, J.A. Reynolds, R.B. Jackson, D.M. Lodge, et al. 2011. "Earth Stewardship: Science for Action to Sustain the Human–Earth System." *Ecosphere* 2, no. 8, pp. 1–20.

[7] Biermann, F., K. Abbott, S. Andresen, K. Bäckstrand, S. Bernstein, M.M. Betsill, H. Bulkeley, et al. 2012. "Navigating the Anthropocene: Improving Earth System Governance." *Science* 335, no. 6074, pp. 1306–07.

[8] Chapin III, F.S., R. Carpenter, G.P. Kofinas, C. Folke, N. Abel, W.C. Clark, P. Olsson et al. 2010. "Ecosystem Stewardship: Sustainability Strategies for a Rapidly Changing Planet." *Trends in Ecology & Evolution*, 25, no. 4, pp. 241–49.

[9] Waddock, S. 2015. " Reflections: Intellectual Shamans, Sensemaking, and Memes in Large System Change." *Journal of Change Management* 15, no. 4, pp. 259–73.

The idea of earth stewardship is one new guiding idea that can power-fully shape mindsets. Earth stewardship is defined as "shaping trajectories of social-ecological change at local-to-global scales to enhance ecosystem resil-ience and human wellbeing."[10] The Earth Stewardship Initiative attempts to integrate science, planning, and designers across multiple disciplines in the interests of promoting ecological resilience and emphasizing the revi-talization of communities at different levels. Fundamental to earth stew-ardship is redefining human beings relationship to the planet, away from separation and exploitation towards the more harmonious, balanced rela-tionship advocated by many Indigenous thinkers.[11] That perspective means bringing human activities into harmony with the natural resources avail-able that can be tapped without harming nature's future ability to replen-ish, renew, restore, and regenerate what is needed for future generations.[12]

Achieving such global stewardship of planetary resources and secur-ing human beings' place on the planet for the future, by whatever name we call it, is of paramount concern in thinking system transformation. Getting there, however, means transformational, change in just about all domains, perhaps most importantly in business practices.

Important to identify in these processes are the relevant values associ-ated with the desired change, some of which will be discussed in the next chapter. These values need to link to the vision, for example, purposes here, a state of well-being and dignity for all in the context of a flourishing ecosystem.

Who Can Undertake Transformation?

Clearly, if humanity is to thrive in the future, a rather massive system change is in order, a transformation away from neoliberalism towards the

---

[10] ESA (Ecological Society of America) Earth Stewardship. 2018. URL: https://esa.org/esa/science/earth-stewardship/

[11] Narvaez, D., Four Arrows (D. Trent Jacobs), E. Halton, B. Collier B., and G. Enderle, eds. 2019. *Indigenous Sustainable Wisdom: First-Nation Know-How for Global Flourishing*. New York, NY: Peter Lang, pp. 27–46. See also Four Arrows (aka Donald Trent Jacobs). 2016. *Point of Departure: Returning to Our More Authentic Worldview for Education and Survival*. Charlotte, NC: IAP.

[12] See: Earth Stewardship, https://earthstewardshipinitiative.com/vision.

life-affirming and flourishing-oriented conception of organizing human systems, which includes a more nature-centric way of thinking about humanity's place in the world. Thinking about businesses in all of these change processes, companies and their leaders will have to shift away from the current obsession with growth (of GDP, of profits, of return to shareholders, of market share, of products/services sold) towards different types of goals. Planetary resources cannot sustain current growth patterns, with human population at this writing at nearly 7.8 billion.[13] Strains on natural resources are already evident with the current population of just over seven billion people.

In this light, a shift of the system to bring about a re-ordering of priorities and incentives for individuals, companies, other institutions, and countries, is necessary. That shift means a rebalancing of interests that the Quechua people in South America call a *Pachakuti*. The Pachakuti "can be interpreted to symbolize a re-balancing of the world through a tumultuous turn of events that could be a catastrophe or a renovation."[14] In a very real way, the wake-up call associated with the 2020 pandemic is such an event.

Perhaps it is too late avoid the "great disruption" or catastrophe that Gilding[15] suggested was likely if system transformation were not achieved in a timely way. But even more important is to avoid the total collapse of the human enterprise predicted by some thinkers and ecologists[16] (some of which is evident in the ongoing pandemic at this writing). To accomplish

---

[13] Worldometer. 2020. https://worldometers.info/world-population/#:~:text= The%20current%20world%20population%20is,currently%20living)%20 of%20the%20world (accessed June 18, 2020).

[14] Thomson, B. 2011. "Pachakuti: Indigenous Perspectives, Buen Vivir, Sumaq Kawsay and Degrowth." *Development* 54, no. 4, pp. 448–54.

[15] Gilding, P. 2011. *The Great Disruption: Why the Climate Crisis Will Bring on the End of Shopping and the Birth of a New World.* New York: Bloomsbury Publishing USA.

[16] Speth, J.G. 2008. *The Bridge at the Edge of the World: Capitalism, The Environment, and Crossing from Crisis to Sustainability.* New Haven, CT: Yale University Press; also Lovelock, J. 2010. *The Vanishing Face of Gaia: A Final Warning.* New York: Basic Books.

these ends, there are several imperatives that need to be pushed forward reasonably quickly to avoid even more problems.

One perspective on who might undertake transformation came from an analysis by Robert Eccles and George Serafeim in 2012, both then at the Harvard Business School. Eccles and Serafeim argued that because the leaders of just 1,000 massive businesses represent half the market capitalization ($32 of about $60 trillion) of the world's some 60,000 public companies, it is this group that needs to develop a changed mindset.[17] John Fullerton, author of *Regenerative Capitalism*,[18] and ecologist Hunter Lovins further argued in describing the current economy, which is dominated by speculative finance as the "degenerative economy," that "It is not an exaggeration to say that one thousand CEOs and perhaps 20 heads of state hold the future of civilization in their hands."[19] As Fullerton and Lovins suggested, if these 1,020 individuals' minds could be focused on creating real system change and true sustainability, or in our terms, flourishing or thriving, initiatives, not only would the world be in a substantially better situation but these companies (and nations) would also become the role models of stewardship needed for the future.

This degree of power in so few hands in a world of seven and a half billion people is a shocking thought. If it were true, it might make the potential for relatively quick and significant system transformation more of a reality and give a possibility of it happening in relatively short order. There is, of course, the minor problem that the notion of heroic leadership implicitly embedded in such a perspective is itself unrealistic given

[17]   Eccles, R.G., and G. Serafeim. 2012. "Top 1,000 Companies Wield Power Reserved for Nations." *Bloomberg, The Grid* http://bloomberg.com/news/2012-09-11/top-1-000-companies-wield-power-reserved-for-nations.html   (accessed September 11, 2012).

[18]   John, J.F. 2015. *Regenerative Capitalism: How Universal Principles and Patterns Will Shape Our New Economy.* Greenwich, CT: Capital Institute, http://capitalinstitute.org/wp-content/uploads/2015/04/2015-Regenerative-Capitalism-4-20-15-final.pdf

[19]   Fullerton, J., and L.H. Lovins. 2013. "Transforming Finance and the Regenerative Economy." Paper prepared for the Tellus-Institute/MIT Sloan Roundtable on "Corporations in a Great Transition." Boston/Cambridge (accessed October 31–November 1, 2013), pp. 19–25, p. 22.

the complexity of the system and the scope and scale of changes needed, as we have discussed. Further, major institutions change slowly if they cannot see the need for change unless disrupted in significant ways— although the pandemic could be said to be doing some of that disrupting. Even if the leaders of these institutions called for changes, it would take time, resources, and the agreement of many, many people in various parts of the system to begin acting. Many leaders are struggling to understand the whole system implications of possible collapse, never mind the implications of things like climate change or ecosystem collapse for their own institutions.

Most likely then, system transformation is not quite as simple as suggesting solely that leaders at the top can effect it. For one thing, changing the mindset of powerful and wealthy adults, who are benefiting from the current system and are effectively indoctrinated with an economic ideology that suggests that markets are infallible and that growth is necessary, is far from easy. For another, there are many other entrenched business, political, and societal interests in addition to this select group of leaders whose minds also have to be changed—and who have to be moved to action.

Highlighting the beginnings of a "new story," in 2019, the CEO-led group the Business Roundtable issued an important statement to "promote an economy that serves all Americans" and generally move the purpose of businesses away from shareholder wealth maximization towards sharing a "fundamental commitment to all stakeholders."[20] The CEOs committed their companies in principle to "delivering value to … customers," "investing in … employees," "dealing fairly and ethically with … suppliers," "supporting the communities in which [their companies] work," and "generating long-term value for shareholders."[21] While it

---

[20] Of course, the foundational perspective on stakeholders comes from Freeman, R.E. 1985. *Strategic Management: A Stakeholder Approach*. Boston: Pitman, a perspective updated in Freeman, R.E., J.S. Harrison, A.C. Wicks, B.L. Parmar and S. De Colle. 2010. *Stakeholder theory: The State of the Art*. Cambridge: Cambridge University Press.

[21] Business Roundtable, Statement on the purpose of a corporation. Business Roundtable. 2019. https://opportunity.businessroundtable.org/wp-content/uploads/2020/04/BRT-Statement-on-the-Purpose-of-a-Corporation-with-Signatures-Updated-April-2020.pdf, (accessed April 17, 2020).

remained to be seen what changes in corporate practice actually happen, the statement represents an important reframing that is fundamental to changing the memes that exist around corporate purposes.

In January 2020, the world's largest asset manager Blackrock's CEO Larry Fink issued an important letter to CEOs of the companies in which Blackrock invests. Citing the protests that had occurred in 2019 around issues of climate change, Fink argued that climate risk is "compelling investors to reassess core assumptions about modern finance" and noted, importantly, that "climate risk is investment risk." Directly addressing current financial narratives that dominate many CEOs thinking, Fink argued that "Our investment conviction is that sustainability –and climate-integrated portfolios can provide better risk-adjusted returns to investors ... [and] we believe that sustainable investing is the strongest foundation for client portfolios going forward." Simultaneously, Fink announced in a letter to clients that the firm was going to "place sustainability at the center of our investment approach."[22] Given Blackrock's power and legacy, one could legitimately be cynical about the extent to which Find's ideas will be taken seriously, but they do point investors in a new and important direction.

Furthermore, during the midst of the Covid-19 pandemic, 12 European Union (EU) environmental ministers appealed to the EU for what they called a "green recovery" from the pandemic, a recovery that would address not just impacts of the virus but also the threats from climate change and sustainability issues facing the world. The EU's Parliament Committee on the Environment subsequently launched a Green Recovery Alliance, a coalition of 79 environmental ministers, and numerous civil society groups, including 37 CEOs, 28 business associations, the European Trade Union Confederation, seven nongovernmental organizations, and six think tanks.[23] In the United States, the "Green New Deal"

---

[22]   Fink, L. 2020. "A Fundamental Reshaping of Finance." *BlackRock*, https:// blackrock.com/corporate/investor-relations/larry-fink-ceo-letter (accessed April 17, 2020).

[23]   Simon, F. 2020. "'Green Recover Alliance' Launched in European Parliament." *Euractiv* (April 14, 2020), URL: https://euractiv.com/section/energy-environment/news/green-recovery-alliance-launched-in-european-parliament/

was launched as a bill in both the House of Representatives and Senate in 2019, but remains stalled at this writing. Despite that outcome, these efforts do represent new thinking on the part of some leaders better able to see the systemic aspects of current crises.

None of these efforts (or numerous others) will be enough to achieve system transformation; however, they do represent some loosening of the hold that neoliberal tenets have had on the finance and business communities, both of which are central to achieving long-term systemic flourishing. For example, Fink could be replaced or retire and his successor might well have a different perspective. System transformation requires system wide efforts that also highlight a key lesson: For system transformation to occur in the context of complex wickedness, most likely means some combination of top-down, bottom-up, and lateral initiatives all geared towards a similar set of objectives around making the world better. In just these three initiatives, we can see efforts from CEOs, an individual CEO, and two legislative efforts, which have been at least in part fueled by massive citizens' protest movements in a wide range of places around the planet and the impact of Covid-19 on human systems.

Transformation needs to be democratized, so that all interested can do their bit, whatever that might be. The ideas about wicked complexity discussed earlier indicate that system transformation can begin anywhere by anyone, assuming it is guided by common goals and values, and appropriate leverage points are used. Transformation needs to involve and engage many, many people in all sorts of capacities in the change process, each doing their own things, hopefully in accord with common visions and values.[24] In other words, the transformation process is a process of social change that needs to involve anyone interested in seeing that change, hopefully positive and constructive, come about. That is where changing the story or narrative comes in, of course. A shared narrative, or perhaps more importantly, shared memes provide common grounding and common sets of goals, values, norms, and practices around which a wide variety of initiatives can potentially coalesce, even if some fail and others go astray. Thus, a pervasive movement needs to be created—top-down,

---

[24]   See, for example, Waddock et al., *The Complexity of Wicked Problems*.

bottom-up, and lateral change initiatives led by many different people with different interests and skills—but aligned around a relatively common agenda—are needed.

Leveraging Memes and Narratives for System Transformation

An important lesson from all of these ideas for change makers is to understand that if change is to occur in the belief system, that is, the cultural myths, narratives, and stories that shape societies and the world, then a resonant alternative needs to replace the old myth so that people understand how to act in the new myth or story.[25] That is why the language, for example, that accompanies Fink's letter is strong in putting forward a new statement about his company's purpose and focus. It is why the meme of a "green new deal" resonated with so many progressive thinkers (despite its lack of success in the U.S. Congress to date)—it draws on the well-understood "New Deal" that helped the United States recover from the Great Depression of the 1930s. It is why the Green Alliance in Europe rapidly gained steam and attention. That put a powerful political organizing strategy behind the initiative.

New memes that reflect the intent and aspirations of the new story/narrative need to be developed and powerfully conveyed, so that others can take up those memes and use them in their own ways. In policy and system contexts, stories and narratives, with their supporting memes, serve a variety of functions. They can influence or engage people; they communicate ideas and ideologies. They tell the structure of a society, organization, or other type of community, so that members can understand the power relationships, structure, and various actors.[26] Similarly, artists of many different arts can create symbols, images, phrases, songs, fiction, nonfiction, poems, paintings, drawings, illustrations, sculptures,

---

[25] McNeill, W.H. 1982. "The Care and Repair of Public Myth." *Foreign Affairs* 61, no. 1, pp. 1–13.

[26] Moezzi, M., K.B. Janda, and S. Rotmann. 2017. "Using Stories, Narratives, and Storytelling in Energy and Climate Change Research." *Energy Research & Social Science* 31, pp. 1–10.

Internet memes, and other pieces of art to convey new ideas, once they begin to be understood broadly. Or, in fact, since artists are frequently visionaries—possibly before the general public catches on.

Given the nature of large system change described earlier, the roles of stories, narratives, and memes, which can include other types of art, in leveraging change should be becoming clear by now. System change, when successful, begins with a new story. In businesses, that story is sometimes called a vision, mission, or purpose. Stories and narratives with strong, resonant memes have the power to shift how people think, even shift their worldview. Indeed, Meadows called the "mindset or paradigm out of which the system—its goals, power structure, rules, its culture—arises"[27] the most powerful lever for system change of the twelve that she initially identified.

In decreasing order of effectiveness, Meadows identified other levers for system change: system goals, power to change the system, rules of the system, structure of information flows, gain around positive feedback loops, strength of negative feedback loops, length of delays in the system, structure of material stocks and flows, sizes of buffers and other stabilizing stocks, and constants, parameters, and numbers.[28] All of these levers are involved in system change at some point, though Meadows said that mindset change, and, a bit later, the ability to transcend mindsets, was the most powerful of all levers. Mindsets are shaped by stories, narratives, ideologies, values, and norms, all of which are comprised of memes.

The lesson for transforming socioeconomic systems is that new memes with the capacity to "infect" and change the old paradigm, substituting for old memes, constituting new and highly resonant stories and narratives are an important first step towards system change. Once new stories are widespread, then all of the other levers of change that Meadows identified can be pulled much more effectively, when they are consonant with the new memes and stories. Since the most effective memes and stories are ones that fall with current understandings and narratives enabling people

---

[27] Meadows, Leverage Points, p. 2.

[28] Donella Meadows, Leverage Points.

to identify with them,[29] the ability to leverage new memes that transcend and include[30] the current narrative may be one key to system change.

To achieve a flourishing world for all, new memes and narratives need to bring together ideas about human beings' place in the natural world, in societies and communities, and, yes, in the enterprises and institutions that form the organized world of human societies. For that to be successful, overarching goals and frameworks are needed, promulgated by powerful institutions and broadly adopted. For example, Kate Raworth has developed her "doughnut economics," which draws on the Stockholm Resilience Centre work, to identify nine geophysical planetary boundaries that cannot be transgressed without significant harm to planetary well-being.[31] On the human or societal side, Raworth then identifies 12 vital aspects of human life that create a social foundation that also needs to be in place to support humanity.[32] This model will be discussed in more detail a bit later. Suffice to say that it presents—in a compelling and easily understandable "doughnut"—or torus-shaped image (a new meme!)—a set of key elements that need to be included in any movement towards holistic well-being for all.

Thus, to move forward proactively means constructing an alternative and inspiring vision to today's dominantly economic one. Because today's dominant neoliberal narrative is an economic one, any new narrative needs to deal with shifting that perspective at least in part by including ideas about what constitutes a successful economy into the new story. This new narrative needs to represent flourishing for all of life, for humans and other living beings, and for human societies and institutions, including

---

[29] Lounsbury, M., and M.A. Glynn. 2001. "Cultural Entrepreneurship: Stories, Legitimacy, and the Acquisition of Resources." *Strategic Management Journal* 22, nos. 6–7, pp. 545–64.

[30] Wilber, K. 2017. "Trump and a Post-Truth World: An Evolutionary Self-Correction." Integral Life URL: https://integrallife.com/trump-post-truth-world/

[31] Johan, R., W. Steffen, K. Noone, Å. Persson, F.S. Chapin III, E. Lambin, T.M. Lenton et al. 2009. "Planetary Boundaries: Exploring the Safe Operating Space for Humanity." *Ecology and Society* 14, no. 2.

[32] Kate, R. 2017. *Doughnut Economics: Seven Ways to Think like a 21st-Century Economist*. White River Junction, VT: Chelsea Green Publishing.

(and transcending) businesses. The next chapter begins to explore what some new memes might be.

An Example of a Guiding Framework: Raworth's Doughnut Economics

As briefly mentioned, Kate Raworth has developed an alternative to current economics that is based on a compelling visual image (a torus that she calls a "doughnut") to argue for new ways to "think like a 21-st century economist" rather than looking backward to the tenets of neoliberalism that frame most economic thinking. Raworth used the Planetary Boundaries work of the Stockholm Resilience Centre as the geophysical set of boundary conditions that humans cannot transgress without endangering civilization on the planet. These boundaries include climate change, ocean acidification, chemical pollution, nitrogen and phosphorous loading, freshwater withdrawals, land conversion, biodiversity loss, air pollution, and ozone layer depletion. Recent work from the Stockholm Resilience Centre suggests that four of these boundaries have already been transgressed.[33]

The real innovation Raworth made in her visually compelling doughnut model (a meme) is to add a middle layer of human needs that must be met for people everywhere to experience wellbeing. These needs include water, food, health, education, income and work, peace and justice, political voice, social equity, gender equality, housing, networks, and energy. If human systems could be redesigned within both sets of boundaries, then what Raworth calls a "safe and just operating system for humanity" would emerge.[34]

---

[33] Jorgen, R., J. Rockström, P.E. Stoknes, U. Goluke, D. Collste, S.E. Cornell, and J. Donges. 2019. "Achieving the 17 Sustainable Development Goals within 9 Planetary Boundaries." *Global Sustainability* 2.

[34] Raworth. 2017.

CHAPTER 6

Emerging a Life-Centered Worldview

Thinking about system transformation is complicated—doing it even more so. System change can occur abruptly when some tipping point is reached and, like natural systems, the system suddenly undergoes a state change—or transformation. Anthropologist Jared Diamond calls such sudden changes in human systems collapse in a book by that title,[1] while author Malcolm Gladwell calls them tipping points, suggesting that small changes in systems can make a big difference.[2] Both of these ideas draw from chaos theory[3] in noting that when systems are at what chaos theorists call the edge of chaos change can happen suddenly. The *global* response to the Covid-19 pandemic certainly demonstrated that type of state change.

As noted, Donella Meadows has pointed towards a number of key leverage points of which mindset change and the ability to transcend mindsets are the most powerful for bringing about system transformation.[4] Five important dimensions of systems provide a potential framework for action: purposes, perspectives, performance metrics, powers, and practices[5] that can be combined with the kind of living systems framework that Raworth provides with her "doughnut." This chapter begins articulating purposes, perspectives, and their

---

[1] Diamond, J. 2005. *Collapse: How Societies Choose to Fail or Succeed.* New York: Penguin, 2005.
[2] Gladwell, M. 2006. *The Tipping Point: How Little Things Can Make a Big Difference.* Boston: Hachette Book Group.
[3] Gleick, *Chaos.*
[4] Meadows, Leverage Points.
[5] Waddock, Achieving Sustainability.

supporting core memes that could potential provide a needed foundation for transformation—shifting power relations and operating practices. The discussion starts with memes of dignity, well-being, flourishing, fulfillment, and connection, recognizing that others may well have different memes they would wish to offer—and in ensuing chapters, I will discuss core ideas about what gives life to systems and the ways in which Indigenous principles of relationship, reciprocity, responsibility, and redistribution might apply to a transformed world. None of us, of course, have all the answers. Gathering and reconciling many different perspectives, through public discourse and dialogue among different communities, institutions, and even nations, and media, artist, and policy engagement, will also be needed.

The task the world faces now and with some urgency is to move away from today's troubled dynamics with its predominantly economic narrative towards a world where humanity lives in harmony with nature, where all living beings receive the dignity that they inherently deserve, and where life flourishes in all respects. To bring this world about, we need a new narrative and a new set of supporting memes (core ideas) that support a positive relationship between humanity and the world around us. The task is nothing less than system change on a massive scale.

In my view, the first step towards this new world is redefining the core purposes of key institutions—including businesses, governments, and schools, among others, to put the well-being of humans *and* all of nature at the center. The new narrative needs to incorporate yet go well beyond business and economic activities, while simultaneously recognizing the fundamental transformations needed in both of those systems. The emphasis needs to be somehow building a world that is more equitable, just, and flourishing for all, defined in whatever terms make sense to people in their particular cultures, traditions, and geographies. Business as usual has created an unsustainable set of ecological conditions in the world, along with gross inequity, and a decided lack of voice or participation by far too many people in public institutions. The new narrative, particularly as the world recovers from the devastation of Covid-19 and attempts to rebuild needs to highlight not business as usual—which is and was highly problematic—but how to rebuild towards a future in which all want and are able to participate equitably—and that also addresses the many ills associated with lack of sustainability. With such a narrative, we can begin to take different courses of action, create new practices, policies, and institutions, and work together towards achieving this vision of greater harmony, less intense resource use, and synergy between humans and nature.

The Power of a New Narrative

Compelling stories, narratives, and visions have a few central characteristic, as expressed by Dagny Scott of Fearless Unlimited: they go beyond "just the facts" and are true, simple, and aspirational.[6] Thus they provide a guide to the future that shows people how all can contribute to that imagined (better) future. In addition, Freya Williams of Futerra notes that to achieve a large system change, you need to combine people and passion and multiply that combination using a compelling a "plot" or story that resonates emotionally with the particular audiences you are interested in reaching.[7] Taken together, this advice suggests that the overarching narrative needs to be general enough to appeal to multiple audiences and allow them to create their own stories specific to their interests, culture, and places, while being specific and aspirational enough to provide hope and some emotional connection to the story that is being woven.

Narratives are foundational in helping people make sense of what is happening and what is expected, providing needed guidance for all who would bring about a change. Narratives and stories can help define purposes and ensure that they are compelling. People do not need to agree on all of the particulars or specifics of the narrative as long as core memes are common. We can contrast a new narrative emphasizing flourishing for all with the neoliberal narrative. The neoliberal narrative, generated by a group of economists, historians, and others after World War II in a

---

[6] Dagny Scott of Fearless Unlimited Expressed these Ideas at the Regenerative Future Summit, Boulder, CO, May 15–17, 2017, URL: https://regenerativefuturesummit.org/dagny-scott/

[7] Freya Williams of Futerra Discussed these Ideas at the Regenerative Future Summit, Boulder, CO, May 15–17, 2017, URL: https://regenerativefuturesummit.org/freya-williams/

meeting in Mont Pelerin, Switzerland,[8] places a couple of important values at its core: freedom and dignity. In the neoliberal narrative, "freedom" means individual freedom for people and companies to do what they want to do as individuals (or individual companies). The fundamental idea is that dignity comes with such freedom. In contrast, in a flourishing for all narrative, individual freedom is important yet it is bounded by the realization that individual freedom can only be achieved in the social and ecological contexts in which we are all embedded and coexist.

This distinction recognizes that humans and many other living beings are social creatures whose freedom inherently depends on collaboration and coexistence with others. It recognizes a concept in African cultures known as *Ubuntu*, the idea that "I am because we are." Thus, freedom is not absolute nor is it something that individual persons or organizations can achieve without regard for others or nature. True freedom occurs when all are flourishing and prospering, where "all" includes not just human beings but also other living beings and nature's ecosystems. To put it bluntly, we are all in this world together and our individual freedom, not to mention our long-term survival as a species, depends intimately on how we live in that context with others.

Other aspects of the neoliberal narrative draw on this individualistic sense of freedom to articulate the need for free markets, where companies and others can do what they like without governmental or other restrictions. In turn, the neoliberal frame advocates free trade across borders, creating a highly competitive environment in which winners tend to take all and to heck with the losers. Rather than viewing governments as providing necessary protections, the neoliberal narrative thus views governments as restrictive, regulations as unnecessary and invasive, and sets forward a belief that the less government there is, the better. Globalization is viewed as part of making progress, with inequality merely an inevitable by-product of competition. If winners and losers are created as part of this process, well, then, so be it. This powerful sense of "less government is better" is what both Ronald Reagan and Margaret Thatcher articulated in the early 1980s, and that messaging has been consistent since. At least

---

[8]   The history is detailed on the Mont Pelerin Society website (undated), URL: https://montpelerin.org/

that was the case until governments were forced to intervene in important ways during the Covid-19 pandemic, when suddenly many people began to remember what governments could and needed to do in times of need—and in public interest.

Other aspects of the neoliberal narrative include an emphasis on constant (economic and material) growth to achieve progress, a belief that is problematic in light of climate change and resource drains now occurring as a result of rapid human population growth. The neoliberal narrative also includes a straightforward notion that progress is based on intense competition among different actors in the system, leaving little room for cooperation or collaboration. Out of this approach also comes the belief that goods and services should be private. In fact, there is a general disregard for public goods in the belief that neither public goods nor the common good of communities are real. Ultimately, this system gets us to today's belief that the sole purpose of companies is to "maximize shareholder wealth." That is, firms exist to serve only one group of stakeholders, the purported "owners" (who actually today may "own" shares only through financial institutions and in broad portfolios so that they do not even know what they own, and often for very short periods of time) rather than the broader set of stakeholders whose interests are invested in the firm. These ideas about individual freedom, free markets, laissez-faire governments, maximized shareholder wealth, progress, and constant growth are the foundational memes on which the neoliberal narrative or story is built.

A new narrative, as developed here, emphasizes connectedness and shared well-being/flourishing, with recognition that both collaboration and competition are necessary. The recognition is that individuals cannot thrive without being in relationship to others. The physical sciences now tell us that at the quantum level everything is connected. The rapid spread of the novel Coronavirus, SARS-Cov-2, globally highlighted the connected nature of today's globalized world, highlighting that in ecosystems, when one part of the system changes, the whole system alters, too. That recognition underlies the need to emphasize connectedness in any new narrative.

The idea of shared flourishing brings back the notion of common good or the public interest/public good, that is, the fundamental notion that we are all in this world together. The exponential rate of human population growth over the past century plus and the consequent straining of ecological resources means there is a need to recognize this idea of common good on a planetary level, not just locally in communities or even nationally. Too many issues like climate change, problems in the oceans or the air, various forms of pollution, pandemics, and many other issues transcend national boundaries today and need to be dealt with at the global level.

Memes "work" when they replicate easily from mind to mind (person to person) and when many people start to use them in similar ways, in effect, telling similar stories. Memes are like viruses that spread among people, suggesting that they are like a contagion[9] when resonant. Such successful memes draw upon people's core values, interests, and understandings, perhaps elaborating or shifting them, but somehow resonating with what is already at least somewhat familiar or in accord with how people see the world.[10] In developing transformational system changes and the stories that guide them, it is important to consider what people are already familiar with, what their values are, and what types of ideas, images, metaphors, and symbols will resonate with them. Neoliberals understood this idea very well in developing their core notions of liberty/freedom and individual responsibility, particularly in the U.S. context.

What is important to understand is that memes serve as the foundation of the stories and narratives that we tell ourselves. Important stories, for example, origin stories and stories about "how things work here," frame the ways that people view the world about them, shaping attitudes, beliefs, and behaviors. That is why the underlying memes in the neoliberal narrative, things like "maximize shareholder wealth" or "free markets," are so important. If we wish to bring about a system change towards a new narrative of well-being and dignity for all, then we need similarly powerful—resonant and replicable—memes to support that story. It is resonant memes on which stories, narratives, and frameworks that shape how people act and what they are and are not willing to believe and do are built.

---

9   Williams, "Management Fashions and Fads."
10 Williams, "Management Fashions and Fads."

If the narrative and its memes tell us that inequality is merely a necessary by-product of economic activity and that constant growth is necessary, no matter the ecological consequences, or that the only purpose of firms is to enrich their shareholders, those ideas have consequences—and they are not all positive. A different narrative that emphasizes the common good or collective value,[11] that tells us that we are both individual and collectively responsible, has different and potentially more salutary consequences. This new story, one of shared well-being, connection with others and with nature, shared responsibility for ourselves and each other, living in harmony with nature's resources, will ultimately be better for humanity than the more unrealistic notions of the neoliberal narrative. Importantly, governmental responses to the Covid-19 pandemic have dramatically shifted thinking in governments and beyond about the potential to simply shift focus—to use money on creating flourishing for all versus simply creating wealth. The choice for flourishing is what Global Ecological Footprint founder Matis Wackernagel calls "one planet prosperity," important because as he notes, we humans have only one planet available.[12]

Moving towards a new story of flourishing for all means fundamentally revising some of the memes that support the old story, not by getting rid of them, rather by including and moving beyond them to broader and more encompassing (and probably somewhat more complex) concepts. Although shifting core memes is vitally important to change processes, the role of memes often goes largely unrecognized.[13] For example, in the neoliberal narrative, the idea (meme) of freedom is strongly associated with *individual* freedom, both for the person and for the individual company. In contrast, in a flourishing narrative, the idea of freedom is linked to the ability to create a flourishing world for all, hence is embedded in a sense of the overall flourishing of both the individual *and* the collective, community, organization, society, or, indeed the whole world. The idea is

---

[11] Donaldson, T., and J.P. Walsh. 2015. "Toward a Theory of Business." *Research in Organizational Behavior* 35, pp. 181–207.

[12] Global Footprint Network. 2020. Website, https://footprintnetwork.org/ (accessed May 6, 2020).

[13] Sandra Waddock, *Reflections*.

one of shared freedom, and, in a sense freedom from the desperation of states like poverty, oppression, and otherwise undignified existence.

The neoliberal narrative is all about the economy and production of wealth, with memes of wealth maximization, free markets and trade, and individual responsibilities and freedoms. In contrast, the emerging flourishing/well-being narrative is about economic, societal, *and* planetary flourishing. It involves business prosperity and flourishing communities sharing collective responsibilities for the good of all, offering dignity for humans in ways that suit their cultural norms and for all other living entities. It affords dignity to planetary and human systems, respected as wholes and valuable in and of themselves. All these things are associated with flourishing for all, that is, principles that give life to systems rather than draining the life out of them.

The idea of shared flourishing on a healthy planet is decidedly different from the neoliberal goal of shareholder wealth maximization in a system of supposedly free markets. Indeed, while markets remain important in a flourishing world, they are not the central element of human and planetary well-being. Further, markets need to be fair for all, not just "free," so that people of different means can access them if they wish. With its emphasis on dignity for all, the new narrative emphasizes that we humans are deeply and inextricably connected with each other and, importantly, with nature; we are not separate and distinct from nature. The purpose of shared flourishing on a healthy planet thus emphasizes our interconnectedness with each other—and with the planet itself, as will be discussed more later.

Indeed, the Global Financial Crisis of 2007–2008 suggests that the dominance of financial interests not to mention financial institutions in societies can have rather dramatically negative impacts. Further, much of the emphasis during the Covid-19 pandemic was on returning the *economy* to its former state rather than thinking about social or ecological restoration—or, more importantly, renewal, though attitudes and practices significantly changed during this latter crisis, opening up the potential for transformation. In a finance-dominated world, goals tend to be the accumulation of wealth for its own sake, rather than being linked to a broader set of more humanistic values that aim towards flourishing and dignity for all. Rather, under the flourishing narrative, markets are there to support nature's flourishing while simultaneously meeting real human needs, not to drive the system. That is also true for finance, which is best viewed as a support function that when properly deployed enhances the ability of enterprises of all sorts to successfully provide needed goods and services.

Performance Metrics for Life- and Flourishing-Centric Narratives

The concept of flourishing or well-being reflects the general condition of a person, group, community, or society, and is associated with a positive condition or state of being or a general state of health (wellness), happiness, and prosperity, even thriving. Flourishing means giving vibrancy and "life" to socioecological systems. The idea of well-being tends to focus on humans and their various communities. Well-being has both subjective and empirically measurable (objective) aspects, both of which are important to a complete understanding. Well-being for humans ensures that they are able to live in dignified, secure, and prosperous ways that support vitality (life) and flourishing human and natural systems. Well-being for the planetary systems that include and transcend human beings means that the whole system is flourishing.

While in some ways "happiness" is associated with well-being, well-being actually has many dimensions, all of which are relevant to a holistic way of thinking about the concept. Clearly, there is a subjective side to well-being, which has received much attention in recent years, revolving around the issue of happiness and self-assessments of what is termed life-satisfaction.[14] Helliwell points out, for example, that notions about subjective well-being go back as far as Aristotle. He quotes Aristotle as defining happiness as "prosperity combined with excellence; or as independence of life, or the secure enjoyment of the maximum of pleasure; or as a good condition for property and body, together with the power of guiding one's property and body and making use of them."[15] Among

---

[14] See, for example, Helliwell, J.F. 2003. "How's Life? Combining Individual and National Variables to Explain Subjective Well-Being." *Economic Modeling* 2, pp. 331–60.

[15] Helliwell. 2003. p. 232, Citing Aristotle, *Rhetoric*, 1360b, pp. 14–23.

the "constituent parts" of subjective well-being that Aristotle notes are: "good birth, plenty of friends, good friends, wealth, good children, plenty of children, a happy old age, and also such bodily excellences as health, beauty, strength, large stature, athletic powers, together with fame, honour, good luck and excellence."[16] Helliwell further explains that Aristotle's view of subjective well-being includes a "lifetime's virtuous activities," with material wealth as a means to well-being, not an end it itself.

Martin Seligman, former president of the American Psychological Association, is the developer of important ideas about positive psychology, or the scientific study of what helps people and their communities thrive. Along with a group of colleagues, Seligman argues that subjective well-being is inherently multidimensional in nature, that is, it is composed of multiple parts. Thus, subjective well-being, for Seligman, cannot be reduced to a single concept like happiness, positive emotion, engagement, meaning or purpose, quality of life, life satisfaction, relationships and social support, accomplishment and competence.[17] Instead, all of these elements combine to constitute subjective well-being. Taken separately, none alone defines well-being.

Seligman puts subjective well-being or what is here called flourishing at the core of his ideas about positive psychology, which is the study of what strengths enable individuals to thrive, lead meaningful lives, and enhance their life and work experiences.[18] Such individual flourishing means being able to develop one's talents to the fullest, build strong and lasting relationships with other people, and meaningfully contribute to society. Through what he calls his PERMA model, Seligman and colleagues synthesize subjective well-being and flourishing as having five individual-level attributes: positive emotion, engagement, relationships,

---

[16]   Helliwell, 2003, p. 232, Citing Aristotle, *Rhetoric*, 1360b, pp. 14–23.

[17]   Indeed, in an extensive review Forgeard, M.J.C., E. Jayawickreme, M.L. Kern, and M.P. Seligman. 2011. Consider the multitude of existing definitions and metrics associated with wellbeing in "Doing the Right Thing: Measuring Wellbeing for Public Policy." *International Journal of Wellbeing* 1, no. 1, pp. 79–106.

[18]   Seligman, M. 2010. "Flourish: Positive Psychology and Positive Interventions." *The Tanner Lectures on Human Values*, p. 31.

meaning, and accomplishment (hence the acronym PERMA).[19] Seligman argues that these five attributes best approximate "what humans pursue *for their own sake.*"[20,21,22]

In developing the idea of well-being, Seligman and colleagues built on the work of Amartya Sen, who developed what he terms a "capabilities approach."[23] In that approach Sen distinguished between "functionings," or those things that people value being able to do, and "capabilities," which are what it is possible for them to do.[24] Martha Nussbaum elaborated Sen's ideas by articulating a working list of capabilities that are foundational to collectively contributing to well-being. Based on extensive empirical work, these capabilities, Nussbaum argues, are vital to human well-being. Nussbaum's (evolving) list of specific capabilities includes life (not dying prematurely), bodily health (including reproductive); bodily integrity (freedom of movement, from assault, to make choices). It also includes the development and expression of the senses, imagination, and thought (freedom to use imagination and though); emotional health (ability to make attachments, freedom from fear and anxiety); practical reason (ability to conceive of "the good," religious freedom, freedom of conscience); personal and political affiliation; relationships with other species and nature; play; and control over one's environment.[25]

---

[19]   Seligman. 2011. "Positive Psychology and Positive Interventions." See also Forgeard et al.

[20]   Forgeard et al., 2011, p. 97.

[21]   Huppert, F.A., and T.T. "So, Flourishing Across Europe: Application of a New Conceptual Framework for Defining Well-Being." *Social Indicators Research* 110, no. 3, pp. 837–61, offer a similar conception of well-being or flourishing at the individual level, which includes 10 "hedonic and eudaimonic aspects of well-being: competence, emotional stability, engagement, meaning, optimism, positive emotion, positive relationships, resilience, self esteem, and vitality" (p. 843).

[22]   See also, Jayawickreme, E., M.J. Forgeard and M.E. Seligman. 2012. "The Engine of Well-Being." *Review of General Psychology* 16, no. 4, pp. 327–42.

[23]   Sen, A. 1999. "Capability and Well-Being." In *The Philosophy of Economics: An Anthology*, ed. Dainel M. Hausman, 30–53. Cambridge, UK: Cambridge University Press.

[24]   Sen, 1993; also *Development as Freedom*. New York: Anchor Books.

[25]   Nussbaum, M.C. 2007. "Human Rights and Human Capabilities." *Harvard Human Rights Journal* 20, pp. 21–24. "Which Builds on Capabilities and Human Rights." *Fordham Law Review* 66, pp. 273–300.

Nussbaum's list of capabilities bridges the individual conception of well-being into systemic and empirically measurable conceptions that work at the system level, which is also important to a fulsome understanding of well-being. It is important to build this bridge because well-being/flourishing occurs not just at the individual level but at numerous collective levels, including family, community, societal, national, and planetary, which is increasingly recognized as important, for example, by governments.

In one important initiative aiming to move the bar on collective well-being, the Organization for Economic Cooperation and Development (OECD), for example, has developed a Better Life Index, a sort of well-being dashboard,[26] to measure societal well-being. The Better Life Index attempts to capture well-being's dimensions, emphasizing four key features: people, that is, individuals and households and their relationships to their communities; aspects that go beyond the purely economic; relative equity of distribution among the populace; and both present and future considerations. The Better Living Index, as described by Romina Boarini and Marco Mira d'Ercole, attempts to put Amartya Sen's "capabilities" approach into practice, emphasizing two key domains: material living conditions and quality of life, which are subcategorized into 11 different dimensions that are considered relevant everywhere.[27]

Specific indicators or dimensions that the OECD views as constituting well-being include and go beyond the subjective experience of well-being, which is only one of 11 dimensions, all of which are considered "universal," or relevant in every nation.[28] The dimensions, reflecting Sen and Nussbaum's capabilities, are:

- Jobs and earnings (that is, command over resources and the ability to develop skills and abilities)
- Housing

---

[26]   As advocated by Marie Forgeard, J.C., E. Jayawickreme, M.L. Kern, and M.E.P. Seligman. 2011. "Doing the Right Thing: Measuring Wellbeing for Public Policy." *International Journal of Wellbeing* 1, no. 1.

[27]   Boarini, R., and M.M. d'Ercole. 2013. "Going beyond GDP: An OECD Perspective." *Fiscal Studies* 34, no. 3, pp. 289–314, pp. 293–94.

[28]   Boarini, Going Beyond GDP, p. 294.

- Health
- Education
- Work–life balance
- Civic engagement
- Social connections
- Environmental conditions
- Personal security
- Subjective well-being

Not surprisingly, of course, the OECD also adds income and financial wealth (i.e., usable financial/economic resources), which, as David Korten points out,[29] is a conflation of money with actual wealth (as opposed to what John Ruskin called "illth," the reverse of wealth[30]).[31]

To support and measure these dimensions of well-being, the OECD has identified 55 specific indicators that are regularly compiled in different nations, come from sources (typically national statistics offices), and allow for disaggregation of different subgroups.[32] Obviously, the complexity of the idea of well-being suggests that no single indicator, no "magic bullet," will be sufficient to understanding well-being. The OECD's Better Life Index and its annual "How's Life" survey, which uses these 11 dimensions to assess and compare well-being across nations, reflect this recognition of the complexity of the concept.[33] The idea is that eight dimensions of quality of life (health status, work and life balance, education and skills, social connections, civic engagement and governance, environmental quality, personal security, and subjective well-being) are assessed against indicators of material conditions (jobs and earnings, and housing, and income and wealth, [important, at least, in how today's wealth, not illth is measured]) to reflect individual well-being. These indicators of the present state of

---

[29]   Personal communication.

[30]   Illth, Wikipedia, 2020. URL: https://en.wikipedia.org/wiki/Illth (accessed June 18, 2020).

[31]   Boarini, Going Beyond GDP, pp. 294–95.

[32]   Boarini, Going Beyond GDP, p. 295.

[33]   Durand, M. 2015. "The OECD Better Life Initiative: How's Life? and the Measurement of Well-Being." *Review of Income and Wealth* 61, no. 1, pp. 4–17.

well-being, along with GDP minus what the OECD terms "regrettables," that is, the negative things that GDP takes into consideration. This combination then results in a future-oriented sense of how well well-being will be sustained over time in terms of four capitals: natural, human, economic, and social capital.

There are other leading candidates for measuring well-being that similarly go beyond gross domestic (national) product (GDP), which has been known to be a flawed metric since its introduction. GDP/GNP measures only economic activity—for good or for ill. Thus, clearcutting a forest, while devastating for the natural environment and many creatures in it, is a boon to GDP. Similarly, if you become ill and go to the hospital, GDP will benefit, even as you suffer from the illness. As then U.S. Senator Bobby Kennedy said in a 1968 speech when he was running for president, GDP "measures everything except that which is worthwhile."[34] To deal with the limitations of GDP and begin to get a handle on measuring well-being, we need new metrics and indicators that subtract the negatives and enhance the positives.

Indicators that address well-being better than GDP does include the Gross National Happiness Index, promoted by the government of Bhutan, the UN's Human Development Index, and the Genuine Progress Indicator. The Gross Happiness Indicator (GNH), developed by his Majesty, the Fourth King of Bhutan, Jigme Singye Wangchuk, in 1972,[35] includes four "pillars" (good governance, sustainable socioeconomic development, cultural preservation, and environmental conservation). It also includes nine domains, which include psychological well-being, health, education, use of time, cultural diversity and resilience, good governance, community vitality, ecological diversity and resilience, and living standards. Some 33 indicators measuring these domains are integrated to develop a single number, which is known as the GNH Index, an index that can be disaggregated to assess the GNH of particular groups for use in policy decisions that hopefully enhance overall well-being.

---

[34]   Kennedy, B. 1968. "University of Kansas." URL: https://theguardian.com/news/datablog/2012/may/24/robert-kennedy-gdp (accessed May 27, 2020).

[35]   Details here are from the Gross National Happiness website: http://grossnationalhappiness.com/ and http://grossnationalhappiness.com/articles/

The United Nations' Human Development Index (HDI) similarly combines a number of elements to construct a single number index, though it is relatively simpler than some of the other well-being metrics. HDI emphasizes three key dimensions, including a long and healthy life (specifically, life expectancy at birth), being knowledgeable (specifically, mean years of schooling for adults over 25 and expected years of schooling for children entering school), and having a decent standard of living (gross national income per capita).[36] As the website admits, however, the HDI is a partial indicator of its intended target of human development, overlooking issues like inequality, poverty, security, and empowerment.

The Genuine Progress Indicator (GPI), like the OECD Better Living Index, is a holistic, complex, and robust treatment of well-being based on the belief that "if policymakers measure what really matters to people—health care, safety, a clean environment, and other indicators of well-being—economic policy would naturally shift toward sustainability."[37] Considered an economic indicator, GPI is meant to replace GDP by providing a more accurate and holistic assessment of the economy that takes into account whether economic activity benefits or subtracts from sustainability and well-being, rather than simply measuring that activity as GDP does. One problem, however, is that GPI begins with the same data that GDP uses, hence it is monetarily based (which can cause "illth" rather than actual wealth or well-being). It adjusts for income distribution; housework, volunteering, and higher education; crime; resource depletion; pollution; long-term environmental damage; changes in leisure time; defensive expenditures; life span of consumer durables and public infrastructure; and dependence on foreign assets.[38] But, problematically for a discussion of well-being (as real wealth), this index is still framed in monetary terms—in a sense buying into the same economic logic that has gotten the world into its current difficulties.

---

[36]   Human Development Index website. 2020. URL: http://hdr.undp.org/en/content/human-development-index-hdi (accessed May 27, 2020).

[37]   Quoting Redefining Progress on the Genuine Progress Indicator, General Agreement on a New Economy, URL: http://greenecon.org/gane/resources/federal/fed_res.php (accessed May 27, 2020).

[38]   General Agreement on a New Economy.

In the overall context of generating well-being, it is becoming increasingly clear to some governments and many other observers that some metric that goes well beyond GDP is needed. The three introduced above illustrate that such metrics exist and can be rigorously developed and employed to provide more complete assessments of how the world is working, in particular, whether humans and other living beings of all sorts are accorded dignity so that they can experience well-being the context of a flourishing natural environment.

Perspectives—Dignity as a Core Value

To have dignity means to have intrinsic worth, worth that has nothing to do with status, rank, wealth, or any other criterion except that one *is*.[39] All humans and other living beings, ecosystems, and planet earth itself need to be accorded dignity. In other words, dignity is accorded to fellow human beings simply because they are, not because of who they are, what they have done, or what they are worth. Dignity scholar and conflict resolution expert Donna Hicks says that dignity and respect need to be differentiated, because all have inherent dignity, while respect is something that must be earned. She further argues that dignity violations are at the heart of most if not all human conflict.[40] Amartya Sen similarly argues that all people ought to be able to use their capabilities to gain adequate functionings, that is, people should have sufficient knowledge, resources, and other necessities, to be able to live in meaningful and dignified ways, as explored above in thinking about well-being.

The concept of dignity is traditionally applied to human beings. Here, though, I want to broaden that concept so that we can more fully develop a perspective that will truly enhance flourishing for all. "All" envelopes other living beings of all sorts and natural ecosystems. In short, to get to a flourishing planet that supports flourishing human existence, new ways to accord dignity to all of nature's creatures and ecological manifestations are vital. Mistreatment of the natural environment and other living

---

[39]   Hicks, D. 2011. *Dignity: The Essential Role It Plays in Resolving Conflict.* New Haven: Yale University Press.

[40]   Hicks, *Dignity.*

beings greatly diminishes how life can flourish in all respects. Nature's manifestations include living beings of all sorts, of course, both plant and animal. That perspective encompasses things like trees, aquatic life, birds, and mammals. It also includes nature's and human beings' systems—forests, rivers, lakes, and oceans, plains, mountains, communities, regions, nations, families, and so on. The idea here is that these ecosystems and the creatures they support have intrinsic worth. They are not valuable simply because they can be exploited by or are useful to humans; instead, they are valuable—and should be accorded dignity—in their own right.

This more universal perspective on dignity recognizes the inherent worth of other creatures and of nature herself, creating a more earth- and life-centric socioeconomic perspective, which is in distinct contrast to traditional Western views that tend to place humankind in the center of things. Such a view accords with emerging systems perspectives from physics that recognize that everything is fundamentally interconnected, including humans with nature. From a practical perspective, since we humans draw all of what we need from nature, it is sheer folly to think that we can strip nature's resources, degrade ecosystems, and abuse natural entities without long-term consequences, some of which we are already facing in the form of climate change and various crises of ecosystem sustainability. While nature may be bountiful enough to support some of that behavior for a time, as human population grows and impacts increase, it becomes quite literally unsustainable. The hard reality is that unless nature's resources are stewarded successfully, human civilization is at severe risk.

Using a dignity lens for all of nature's manifestations—people, other living beings, and ecosystems—is entirely consistent with many Indigenous perspectives, which view manifestations of nature as having spirit[41] and hence worthy of being accorded dignity, will be discussed in the next

---

[41]   Four Arrows Jacobs, D.T. 1986. *Point of Departure: Returning to Our More Authentic Worldview for Education and Survival*, Charlotte, NC: Information Age Publishing, 2016; and Dow, J. 1986. "Universal Aspects of Symbolic Healing: A Theoretical Synthesis." *American Anthropologist* 88, no. 1, pp. 56–69.

chapter.[42] It also has significant implications for how we humans treat each other, not to mention the way our businesses and other institutions deal with the raw materials that nature provides and the waste that is created in production processes. Such a dignity lens also recognizes the interconnectedness of all of life and, in a sense, the "oneness" of humans with the rest of the earth and even the universe itself, bringing forward the type of conception of our planet expressed by James Lovelock as the living system, Gaia.[43]

The next chapter looks at how focusing on flourishing—or what gives life to systems—can help move societies toward creating what has been called collective value.

---

[42]   See Waddock, S. 2019. "Wisdom, Sustainability, and the Intellectual Shaman." In *Sustainable Wisdom: Integrating Indigenous Knowhow for Global Flourishing*, eds. D. Narvaez, B. Collier, Four Arrows, E. Halton, R. Nozick and G. Enderle, pp. 244–64. New York: Peter Lang.

[43]   Lovelock, J.E. 1979. *A New Look at Life on Earth*, Oxford University Press, 1979 and *The Vanishing Face of Gaia: The Final Warning*, PublicAffairs.

CHAPTER 7

Towards Flourishing Life and Creating Collective Value

Developing flourishing, life-oriented socioeconomic systems means understanding what it is that allows systems to flourish and moving towards outcomes that enhance what scholars Tom Donaldson and Jim Walsh have called collective value (without any dignity violations). This chapter develops these ideas in more depth, starting with a discussion of flourishing built on understanding Indigenous wisdom and exploring what gives life to systems. Then the chapter moves towards an examination of collective value based on important work by Thomas Donaldson and James Walsh.

Flourishing

Flourishing encompasses and goes beyond the idea of sustainability, which really means to maintain in a steady state. In other words, there is a sense in which despite the best intentions of users of the word sustainability, it really has connotations of continuing business as usual. As has been discussed already, business as usual is highly problematic—and even unlikely in the aftermath of the Covid-19 pandemic. Flourishing, in going beyond sustainability, means to thrive or to have vigorous and healthy growth (which, in contrast to neoliberalism, does *not* mean endless economic growth but rather growth in diversity or abundance, that is, in complexity of a system). Flourishing comes from the idea of abundance found in healthy natural settings. Indeed, the root of the word *flourish* comes from the Old French word *floriss*, meaning to flower. Indigenous wisdom integrally understands the need for flourishing human and natural ecosystems.[1] Flourishing is what German biologist Andreas Weber calls "enlivenment"[2] and my collaborator Petra Kuenkel and I defined as "what gives life to systems."[3]

Indigenous Worldviews: Relationship, Responsibility, Reciprocity, Redistribution

Many Indigenous peoples lived in harmony with their place—the natural environment—for long periods of time, which is not to say there were not some destructive practices. On the whole, however, as archeologist Penny Spikins points out in a book on *Indigenous Sustainable Wisdom*, "A record of strength through *interdependence on each other* in our distant past is far more extensive and compelling than that for aggression or competition."[4] Indigenous worldviews are articulated in numerous books by Native American scholar Four Arrows (aka Donald Trent Jacobs).[5]

Building on this perspective, in a paper Edwina Pio and I[6] draw from work by Harris and Wasilewski who argue that across many Indigenous cultures, four key values of relationship, responsibility, reciprocity, and redistribution are core values that contribute to flourishing or thriving communities. The a key thing to note here is that these values are ancient and found in many, many cultures, including many Eastern and Southern

---

[1] Ideas about Indigenous wisdom are drawn from Pio, E., and S. Waddock. 2020. *Invoking Indigenous Wisdom for Management Learning.* Management Learning, in press 2020.

[2] Weber, Enlivenment.

[3] Ideas about "what gives life to systems" are drawn from two papers: Waddock, S., and P. Kuenkel. May 2019. "What Gives Life to Large System Change?" *Organization and the Natural Environment*, DOI: https://journals.sagepub.com/doi/10.1177/1086026619842482, and Kuenkel, P., and S. Waddock. 2019. "Stewarding Aliveness in a Troubled Earth System." *Cadmus* 4, no. 1, pp. 14–38.

[4] Spikins, P. 2019. "What Can Ancient Hunter-Gatherers Tell us About Sustainable Wisdom?" In *Indigenous Sustainable Wisdom: First-Nation Know-how for Global Flourishing*, Narvaez, D., Four Arrows (Trent Jacobs, D.), Halton, E., Collier B., and Enderle, G, eds. 27–46, p. 31. New York, NY: Peter Lang.

[5] See, for example, Four Arrows (aka Donald Trent Jacobs), *Point of Departure.*

[6] Pio and Waddock, *Invoking Indigenous.*

cultures as well as Indigenous ones. (They are also present in Western/ Northern cultures, but are not necessarily as dominant.) What is also notable is how different these values are from the values of individual (and company) freedom, a clear orientation towards the primacy of markets, (financial) wealth building, and continual growth, among others, that are core values in the neoliberal model that frames today's Northern, industrialized economies (and societies), discussed earlier.

The idea of relationship, which resonates with the Buddhist philosophy of being in "right relationship," is expressed in U.S. Native American tradition by the Lakota phrase *Mitakuye Oyasin*, which translates as "We are all related" (or "All are related"). The meaning of relationship in this tradition is profound, in that the phrase really signifies that the "we" means all of the beings on the Earth—not just humans. This "we" includes marine species, animals, winged beings including insects and birds, trees, and other plants, and even the lakes, rivers, streams, rocks, and mountains of which the world is made. Contrast that perspective to the dominant perspective in the Western world that nature and her beings are there for exploitation—domination—by humans. This value sets up a very different relationship with nature—one of interconnectedness, and recognition of interdependence. While it does not mean that humans cannot use nature's bounty at all, it does suggest a very different attitude towards its use—one away from dominance and exploitation and towards respect for the sacredness, worth, and, indeed, dignity of all beings.

The idea of a relational—interconnected—way of being in the world is part of a holistic, integral worldview, according to Four Arrows.[7] From this perspective or worldview, humans cannot (and should not) consider themselves separate from nature. As thought leader and author David Korten frequently writes, "We are living beings born of a living planet and we forget that at our peril."[8] If we think about an economy that supports life and flourishing for all, the idea of relationship (connectedness) needs to be a central component of that thinking.

---

[7] Four Arrows (aka Donald Trent Jacobs), *Point of Departure*.

[8] Korten, D. Fall 2017. "Ecological Civilization and the New Enlightenment." *Tikkun* 70, pp. 16–23.

Another important value across many Indigenous cultures is that of responsibility, which unlike the individual sense of responsibility in neoliberalism, is defined as responsibility to the community and particularly to the land or place where people reside.[9] Responsibility so defined is another form of connection—a spiritual and collective connection that hold responsibility for ancestral lands and the natural environment, and the communities supported by them, as sacred. Such thinking is frequently expressed in the Native American Iroquois Nation's idea of thinking through the implications of any decision for seven generations out.[10]

A third value frequently found in Indigenous cultures is that of reciprocity or the recognition of mutual benefit that comes from granting privileges or exchanges from person to person or group to group. Reciprocity implies mutual dependence—interdependence—and helping others while knowing that they will also help in return when there is need. The pan-African notion of *Ubuntu*, "I am because we are" embeds this notion of reciprocity and illustrates how important it is to shaping the identity of community members—because they see themselves as part of a broader collective rather than individuals. Similar collective understandings of identity are found in many Eastern and Southern cultures as well. A dominant idea in Western thought, expressed as a core aspect of neoliberalism, has tended to be that of individual identity and in some cases rather extreme individualism,[11] as if one person could exist separately from others. The idea of reciprocity in Indigenous cultures highlights the relationships among humans and also between humans and nature, as a reflection of the understanding of natural processes as cyclical or circular, rather than linear. Reciprocity embeds the idea of balance, too, since there

---

[9] Harris, L.D., and J. Wasilewski. 2004. "Indigeneity, an Alternative Worldview: Four R's (Relationship, Responsibility, Reciprocity, Redistribution) vs. two P's (Power and Profit). Sharing the Journey Towards Conscious Evolution." *Systems Research and Behavioral Science: The Official Journal of the International Federation for Systems Research* 21, no. 5, pp. 489–503.

[10] Kawamoto, W.T., and T.C. Cheshire. 2004. "A 'Seven-Generation' Approach." *Handbook of Contemporary Families: Considering the Past, Contemplating the Future*, pp. 385–93. Thousand Oaks, CA: Sage.

[11] For interesting background, see the work of Lodge and Vogel, *Ideology and National Competitiveness*.

is an understanding that, in a sense, what goes around comes around. Reciprocity, which reflects holistic thinking, emphasizes caring and, as the fourth value, redistribution, indicates, also sharing as mutual obligations that exist among living beings as part of a bigger whole.[12]

The fourth value mentioned by Harris and Wasilewski is that of redistribution. Redistribution is the "sharing obligation" whose purpose is to "balance and rebalance relationships."[13] Indeed, the whole idea of wealth, which is part of the idea of redistribution—sharing one's wealth—is different in most Indigenous cultures from the emphasis on financial wealth that is pervasive in today's economic thinking. Native American scholar Stephanie Gutierrez discusses the Lakota understanding of wealth as not based in financial wealth but rather in living by community virtues with the objective of living a happy, well-balanced life. She points out that the important goal is that of caretaking and ensuring the well-being of future generations.[14]

Interestingly, the idea of relationship is central to all four of these concepts. Relationship is the core—and the other values of responsibility, reciprocity, and redistribution all serve to enhance the quality of the connections in the context of the community. Since physicists now tell us that the universe is highly connected at the quantum level and ecologists let us know that ecologies are connected wholes, it seems more than reasonable that a flourishing, life-centric socioeconomy would also emphasize the importance of relationships and connectedness.

---

[12]   Narvaez, D., Four Arrows, E. Halton, B. Collier and G. Enderle, eds. 2019. "People and Planet in Need of Sustainable Wisdom." In *Indigenous Sustainable Wisdom: First-Nation Know-How for Global Flourishing*, 1–24. New York, NY: Peter Lang.

[13]   Harris, L.D., and J. Wasilewski. 2004. "Indigeneity, An Alternative Worldview: Four R's (Relationship, Responsibility, Reciprocity, Redistribution) vs. Two P's (Power and Profit). Sharing the Journey Towards Conscious Evolution." *Systems Research and Behavioral Science: The Official Journal of the International Federation for Systems Research* 21, no. 5, pp. 489–503, p. 493.

[14]   Gutierrez, S. 2018. "An Indigenous Approach to Community Wealth Building: A Lakota Translation." Washington. DC: Democracy Collaborative. https://community-wealth.org/sites/clone.community wealth.org/files/downloads/Community WealthBuildingALakotaTranslation-final-web.pdf (accessed April 13, 2019).

Giving Life to Systems

Understanding how systems flourish means understanding what it is that gives "life" to systems, or what architect Christopher Alexander called the "quality without a name,"[15] which might be called aliveness, vitality, or vibrancy. Building from work that Petra Kuenkel and I did, this section outlines the principles that we believe give life to systems and, in particular, socioeconomic systems.[16] Six key aspects of systems that, combined and integrated, offer the potential for flourishing, slightly reframed, are: purpose or intentionality, interconnectedness, diversity, boundedness or containment, novelty, and wholeness based on reciprocity. A seventh characteristic specific to human systems is consciousness or awareness, which can be used to design better or flourishing systems into the future.

Living systems have a purpose or what we labeled intentional generativity. Sometimes that purpose is as simple as an instinct to survive[17] and sometimes in socioeconomic systems, including organizations and even whole societies, purpose is more intentionally framed and generated. In human systems, purpose can give meaning to participants in systems, and provide a framework around which their work, ideas, and play can revolve. The idea of generativity is important, too, because it implies a need for flourishing or going beyond what already exists to some new, hopefully better state. The idea of regenerative systems embraces this characteristic of aliveness in flourishing systems, because it follows important ecological principles that McDonough and Braungart articulated in their book *Cradle to Cradle*, that is, the idea that "waste equals food." In other words, in naturally alive systems, nothing goes to waste because what is waste for one part (holon) in the system becomes food for other parts (holons) in the system.[18] For human or socioeconomic systems, the idea of purposes

---

[15] Alexander, C. 1979. *The Timeless Way of Building*. New York: Oxford University Press.

[16] Ideas in this section come from: Waddock and Kuenkel, "What Gives Life to Large System Change?" and Kuenkel and Waddock. "Stewarding Aliveness in a Troubled Earth System."

[17] Weber, Enlivenment.

[18] McDonough, W., and M. Braungart. 2010. *Cradle to Cradle: Remaking the way we make things*. New York, NY: MacMillan.

can be powerfully fraught with emotional content that helps cohere people in the system around their shared purposes, ideals, or values, allowing them to exert their collective strength in ways that enhance flourishing in the system.

Another principle identified (in no set order, by the way) is that of connectedness (what we called contextual interconnectedness), which resonates well with the Indigenous values around relationship discussed above. Physicists like Fritjof Capra now know that life is a highly connected "web" in which different parts are "entangled" with others (both at the quantum level and in ecological settings).[19] From the perspectives of complexity and theories in which this thinking is embedded, life exhibits qualities of emergence, patterns, fundamental unpredictability, and entanglement in which networks of different entities are in constant interaction. That entanglement or connectedness is why systems need to be considered as wholes, rather than fragmented into their parts—because such fragmentation fundamentally damages the integrity that constitutes the system.

The principle of boundedness or what we called permeable containment is also important in determining what gives life to systems.[20] For something to be considered a system, it needs to have boundaries that "contain" and give it some sort of identity and shape. But alive systems also need a degree of permeability, so that new resources, for example, food in biological systems, and ideas, energy, new participants, or other resources in socioeconomic systems can enter sometimes. Permeable boundaries also permit systems to get rid of elements that are no longer useful or needed, that is, waste or excess. Sometimes it is at the boundaries

---

[19] Fritjof Capra has laid out many related ideas in several works: Capra, F. 1995. *The Web of Life*. New York, NY: Doubleday, A. 1995; Capra, F. "Complexity and Life." *Theory, Culture and Society* 22, no. 5, pp. 33-44; Capra, F. 1983. *The Turning Point: Science, Society, and the Rising Culture*. New York: Bantam. Capra, F., and P. Luisi. 2014. *The Systems View of Life: A Unifying Vision*. Cambridge, UK: Cambridge University Press.

[20] For example, see Swanson, G.A., and J.G. Miller. 2009. "Living Systems Theory." *Systems Science and Cybernetics: Synergetics* 1, 136–48. Also Capra and Luisi, *The Systems View of Life*.

where what John Fullerton calls "edge effect abundance" takes place,[21] for it is at the edges where the new energy and ideas come from, while still maintaining the identity of the system.

Another principle that is important in living systems, related in some ways to the idea of boundedness, is that living systems need novelty (we called it emerging novelty). Novelty means that because of new inputs, exchanges, and waste, along with activity within them, systems are constantly changing. Flourishing systems have a tendency to grow more complex (seemingly thwarting the second law of thermodynamics, although some energy is in fact dissipated), even when they do not grow in size, because of the novelty that gets generated within them.[22] The idea of novelty in systems means that they are "enlivened" to use Andreas Weber's term, in an emergent and self-constructive process sometimes called *autopoiesis*.[23]

Diversity[24] or what we called requisite diversity (enough diversity) is an important principle at the core of what gives abundance and the sense of vitality to systems, that in our papers Petra Kuenkel and I linked to connectedness.[25] Requisite diversity allows for system resilience in the face of crises or stress, while insufficient diversity makes the system more

---

[21]   Fullerton, J. 2015. "Regenerative Capitalism: How Universal Principles and Patterns Will Shape Our New Economy." Capital Institute http://capitalinstitute.org/wp-content/uploads/2015/04/2015-Regenerative-Capitalism-4-20-15-final.pdf (accessed May 27, 2020).

[22]   See, for example, Weber, A. 2016. Aliveness. *Biopoetics, in Biosemiotics Series*, Ch. 11, pp. 117–24, Dordrecht: Springer, and Weber, Enlivenment, along with Capra and Luisi. 2014. *The Systems View of Life*.

[23]   Maturana, H.R., and F. Varela. 1987. *The Tree of Knowledge: The Biological Roots of Human Understanding*. Boulder, CO: New Science Library/Shambhala Publications.

[24]   Holling, C.C. 1973. "Resilience and Stability of Ecological Systems." *Annual Review of Ecological Systems*, 4, pp. 1–23; also, Folke, C., S.R. Carpenter, B. Walker, M. Scheffer, T. Chapin, and J. Rockström. 2010. "Resilience Thinking: Integrating Resilience, Adaptability and Transformability." *Ecology and society* 15, no. 4.

[25]   In our papers, Petra Kuenkel and I linked diversity with connectedness, but here I separate it out because it is an important aspect of thinking about what makes systems "come alive."

vulnerable to collapsing or undergoing what complexity theorists call sudden state change.[26] Not only are healthy living systems highly inter-connected, they also have many different elements—diverse species in ecological systems or, in urban designer Jane Jacobs' thinking, in suc-cessful cities diverse types of activities and enterprises that provide both variety and interest to engage people in different ways.[27]

The principle of wholeness, that is, that systems must be considered as wholes rather than broken apart (which kills a living system), was dis-cussed above in the context of the Indigenous concept of reciprocity and is also related to the idea of connectedness. In whole living systems, the parts constitute a living whole that has integrity in and of itself[28]—as itself, even when it made up of holons (parts within wholes),[29] as dis-cussed earlier. The physicist David Bohm called this sense of wholeness the "implicate order" and argued that the very idea of aliveness comes directly from this sense of wholeness. In some ways, it might be said that the idea of transcendence and achieving "oneness" with the universe (by whatever name a higher power goes by in your tradition) builds on this very concept of wholeness.

If we are thinking about how to design socioeconomic systems so that they flourish, we could do worse than to draw on these principles that give life to systems: purpose, boundedness, novelty, connectedness, diversity, and wholeness. When life-giving characteristics are linked with Indigenous ideas that allow particularly human societies to thrive over long periods of time—ideas of relationship, responsibility, reciprocity, and redistribution, they constitute a set of characteristics and attributes that provide a sound basis for developing systems in which people—and all other living beings on the planet—can potentially flourish.

---

[26] Maturana and Varela, *The Tree of Knowledge*.

[27] Jacobs, J. 1961. *The Death and Life of Great American Cities*. New York: Vintage.

[28] Swanson, G.A., and J.G. Miller. 2009. "Living Systems Theory." *Systems Science and Cybernetics: Synergetics*, 1, pp. 136–48.

[29] See also Fullerton. 2016. "Regenerative Capitalism; Andreas Weber, Alive-ness." *Biopoetics, in Biosemiotics Series*, Ch. 11 Dordrecht: Springer, 117–24.

Systemic Flourishing: Creating Collective Value

The perspectives and the principles outlined above drive towards system flourishing. They do set out a big task, however, and it is one that requires decision makers in any capacity to take stewardship of the whole system (or set of systems) in which they are involved. Such a perspective is necessary in a future that deals much more effectively than our current system has done with crises like pandemics—and actually helps humankind cope with even more threatening existential crisis posed by climate change and the potential for ecosystem collapse.

Building these ideas into enterprises and socioeconomic systems could ensure that leaders take responsibility not just for their own enterprise (whether it is a business, governmental agency, legislative body, civil society organization, or some other organization), but also for the welfare of future beings.[30] This idea of stewardship or responsibility for the whole and for the future is a very different concept than many decision makers are used to. It is far more encompassing and demands wisdom, or as scholar Russell Ackoff once defined wisdom, the ability to think through the future and systemic consequences of decisions.[31] The problem that many companies and other institutions have with taking stewardship for the flourishing of the whole and moving towards the expanded set of values discussed above is that today's corporate and institutional purposes tend to be narrowly defined, and do not really take into account the systemic consequences of decisions.

Companies, in particular, are subject to this narrowness of focus, although it also afflicts many governmental leaders. For companies, too

---

[30]   I have articulated these ideas in two papers: "Leadership Ethics for a Troubled World: Responsibility for the Whole." In *Ethical Business Leadership in Troubling Times*, Joanne Ciulla, and Tobey K. Schading, eds. pp. 205–21. Northampton, MA and Cheltenham, UK: Edward Elgar Publishing, and "Stewardship of the Future: Large System Change and Company Stewardship." In *Corporate Stewardship*, E. Lawler, S. Mohrman, and J. O'Toole, eds. pp. 36–54. Sheffield, UK: Greenleaf.

[31]   Ackoff, R. 1996. "On Learning and the Systems that Facilitate It." *Reflections* 1, no. 1, pp. 14–24, reprinted from The Center for Quality of Management, Cambridge, MA.

many people believe that their purpose can be subsumed by the phrases "make profits" or "maximize shareholder wealth," as the neoliberal framing would have it. While legal scholar Lynn Stout argued that there is actually no law, even in the United States, that mandates such a narrow definition,[32] the powerful neoliberal narrative has embedded that type of thinking deeply in many people's psyches and in many legal interpretations as well. That understanding is particularly prominent in the U.S. state of Delaware, where many corporations are officially headquartered. Counter to Stout's view, some legal interpretations suggest that Delaware law, which influences corporate law throughout the United States and elsewhere, does in fact mandate shareholder primacy, despite reality that that norm "is responsible for substantial suffering and political dysfunction in our society," and that "The justifications that its supporters offer on its behalf are implausible."[33]

In the context of neoliberalism, in fact, even many public institutions seem to have lost their "public good" orientation, implicitly adopting Margaret Thatcher's view that, "There is no such thing as society."[34] If there is no such thing as society, there is no shared, common, or public good, and therefore companies and other institutions have no responsibility for the well-being of the whole, this line of thinking goes. With such thinking, businesses in particular are then free to do whatever it takes to make profits while avoiding any responsibility for what economists call "externalities" or side-effects of doing so.

Combine this thinking with the size and impacts of today's multinational corporations, which control immense wealth and command over many markets. One study comparing revenues between the world's countries (taxes) and companies (income) found that of the 100 largest

---

[32] The late Lynn Stout, a legal expert, argued this point in "Why We Should Stop Teaching *Dodge v. Ford.*" *Virginia Law and Business Review*, 2008, 3, pp. 163–427; and *The Shareholder Value Myth: How Putting Shareholders First Harms Investors, Corporations, and the Public*, San Francisco: Berrett-Koehler.

[33] Yosifon, D.G. 2013. "The Law of Corporate Purpose." *Berkeley Business Law Journal* 10, no. 2, pp. 181–230, p. 226.

[34] Cited in Wikiquotes, Margaret Thatcher, https://en.wikiquote.org/wiki/Margaret_Thatcher (accessed April 30, 2019).

"economies" in the world only 29 were nations, while 71 were corpora-tions.[35] Similar findings have been relatively consistent for many years, despite differences in methodologies (and some contestation of the con-cept of comparing these different types of entities).

Dangerously to the idea of common good, at least in the United States, corporations are accorded the privilege of personhood, with atten-dant free speech rights. That combination of rights gives corporations vast privileges and powers that can mean that their negative impacts are not easily checked. Further, in the United States, the Supreme Court's 2010 decision in the *Citizens United v. Federal Election Commission* case, the Supreme Court (controversially) granted corporations the right to free speech, with the implications that they could not be restricted from making political campaign contributions or making independent expen-ditures for related communications.

In the context of these enormous powers combined with the transpar-ency provided by the Internet, businesses have turned towards corporate (social) responsibility in large numbers. The advent of the Internet with its immediate ability to connect people globally and the transparency it provides wittingly or not to corporate actions. Still, it is increasingly clear that the impact of corporate social responsibility (CSR) is on the mar-gins at best and that more fundamental actions that deal with corporate purpose are needed to begin the process of transformation. To move the system to systemic flourishing—that is, whole system health and well-being with dignity for all, core humanistic management values— requires major shifts businesses and their purposes. Businesses are today's dominant institutions, with many controlling more resources than many countries,[36] and so they have huge ecological and social impacts. Even in the wake of the pandemic, despite all of the losses, it is likely that unless significant reframing begins to happen, businesses will retain their predominance as world actors.

---

[35] Babic, M., E. Heemskerk and J. Fichtner. 2018. "Who is More Powerful— States or Corporations?" *The Conversation*, URL: https://theconversation.com/ who-is-more-powerful-states-or-corporations-99616 (accessed April 24, 2020).
[36] Khanna, P. 2016. "Rise of the Titans." *Foreign Policy* 217, pp. 50–55.

Still, the idea of flourishing is increasingly being applied at the organizational level as well as to individuals and entire ecosystems like economies and natural contexts. In a book titled *Flourishing Enterprise*, Chris
Laszlo and Judy Sorum Brown with a number of others focus on flourishing at the organizational level. It is this notion of flourishing that needs to
be built into enterprises of all kinds, if humanity is to thrive in the long
term.[37] Similarly with Andreas Rasche, I argued in *Building the Responsible Enterprise: Where Vision and Values Add Value* that responsibilities of
companies need to be deeply embedded in their strategies, goals, business
models, and practices.[38]

The idea of flourishing as applied to businesses goes well beyond
today's notion of corporate social responsibility or corporate responsibility (CSR/CR). Despite many years of work by companies and scholars
alike, CSR still tends to be an "add on" to corporate strategies, goals,
and practices, rather than integrally related to how business is done. The
idea of flourishing and responsible enterprises really means integrating
and embedding true sustainability and responsibility considerations into
all company activities and impacts on stakeholders and the natural environment alike. Then it means going beyond those activities to take into
account the flourishing of the natural environment in which all else sits.
Getting there requires transformation both of the companies, and as will
be explored a bit later, the ecosystem that surrounds them.

In other words, the idea of flourishing, as we use it here, means that
the whole system is flourishing—not just individual companies within
it. The flourishing of companies is significantly related to and dependent
on the flourishing of the communities of stakeholders that support and
enable that company to exist in the first place, a linkage commonly unrecognized. The core of applying relational values to enterprises of all sorts
means establishing the reality of the connectedness among different types

---

[37]   Laszlo, C., J. Brown, J. Ehrenfeld, M. Gorham, I. Barros-Pose, L. Robson, R.
Saillant, D. Sherman and P. Werder. 2014. *Flourishing Enterprise: The New Spirit
of Business*. Stanford: Stanford Business Books.
[38]   A similar approach is taken by Waddock, S., and A. Rasche. 2012. *Building the Responsible Enterprise: Where Vision and Values Add Value*. Stanford, CA:
Stanford University Press.

of institutions. From the perspective of systems theory and the principles that give life discussed earlier, we cannot tease one element of the whole system apart from others without damaging both the entity itself and the rest of the system. At some level, we need to consider the health, well-being, and flourishing of the whole system in order to gain the necessary perspective.

Shifting companies towards a more balanced perspective fundamentally means rethinking their core purposes and reorienting them towards different ways of dealing with people. Companies need to be seen and recognized as products of their stakeholders and communities—and subordinate to them, rather than (as today) the dominant institution in society. Then stakeholders can retain their dignity and well-being, and the natural environment can retain its capacity to restore, replenish, regenerate, and renew itself, providing natural resilience that helps support the human enterprise. The risk of not doing so is not that the planet or the natural environment will not survive. Rather the risk is that human beings and their civilizations may not be able to thrive into the future—or if they do, that it will be in much diminished ways.

What, then, creates the systemic integrity and flourishing needed to ensure a better future for humanity, for its business and other enterprises, and ultimately for all living beings? Thinking through the values from Indigenous wisdom and principles that give life, discussed earlier in this chapter, provides many clues. It is important to recognize that while vitally important to meeting human needs and desires, businesses are only one aspect of the whole system. Businesses are integrally tied to natural resources, as they cannot survive without somehow drawing from those natural resources. They are equally tied to the efforts of employees and the families who support and nurture those employees, and the communities in which they live. Governments set up the conditions under which businesses operate—the rules of the game, in a sense—ensuring that (at least when things are working well) there is a level-playing field.

Businesses, governments, civil society, and the natural environment, along with other important aspects of the system, for example institutions that support and enhance spirituality, civic and activist organizations, educational institutions at all levels, health care institutions, and other human institutions are all bound together into a whole. They are connected, and those connections can either support flourishing or, when they are fragmented and broken, destroy it. The idea of transformation built on values that support flourishing is to create a healthy set of connections, supported by clear recognition that the well-being of the whole is dependent on the well-being of all of the parts.

Accomplishing these goals requires major shifts. First of all, it requires reframing how the purposes of businesses are understood and addressing the core purposes of businesses as they operate in societies—thereby influencing and changing perspectives or mindsets. It means shifting the metrics by which businesses and whole economies, are evaluated, which requires massive system transformation. It means restructuring firms so that they are no longer have incentives to act as psychopaths, as lawyer Joel Bakan called them in his important book *The Corporation*.[39] Instead, they need to be designed for social and ecological resilience following a set of principles outlined by Tellus Institute's Allen White in an initiative called Corporation2020.[40] These principles orient companies towards harnessing private interests to serve the public interest, balancing all stakeholders' interests (not prioritizing shareholders), operating sustainable, distributing wealth equitably, and not infringing on natural persons' human rights or the right to govern themselves. Then it means applying the same principles of humanism and what gives life to all of society's institutions.

Beyond individual and organizational flourishing and well-being, as noted in discussing well-being earlier, there is another, more collective and systemic use of the term. At the system level, flourishing refers to overall sustainability and systemic health, prosperity, and well-being. In that usage, it relates to ecological and systemic sustainability, as discussed by John Ehrenfeld and Andrew Hoffman in their book titled *Flourishing*.[41] These authors argue that human systems need to be radically shifted towards more ecological sustainability if humans are to thrive into the

---

[39] Bakan, Joel. *The Corporation: The Pathological Pursuit of Profit and Power.* New York: Simon and Schuster.

[40] Corporation2020. Corporation2020: Designing for Social Purpose. 2020. https://corporation2020.org/ (accessed June 18, 2020).

[41] See, for example, Ehrenfeld, J. and A. Hoffman. 2013. *Flourishing: A Frank Conversation about Sustainability.* Palo Alto: Stanford University Press.

future. There needs to be a shift away from today's materialism, consumerism, and growth spirals towards more satisfying and meaningful ways of interacting with other humans and with the planet itself.

Accomplishing this task inherently means shaping new metrics at both the national level, as discussed earlier, and at the individual company or the institutional level, with an emphasis on generating not simply individual company value or wealth maximization but towards a broadened definition of collective value.[42] Major policy shifts in how the purposes of businesses and other institutions are defined will be needed—hence the need for mindset shift discussed in the last chapter. One idea that has potential is to think about enterprises of all sorts, whether for-profit, not-for-profit, NGOs, or governmental, creating what has been called collective value.

Performance Metrics: Collective Value(s)

Thomas Donaldson and James Walsh introduced the idea of collective value as the fundamental purpose of business in pathbreaking research,[43] in which they developed a theory of business. Donaldson and Walsh define business as "a form of cooperation involving the Production, Exchange and Distribution of goods and services for the purpose of achieving Collective Value."[44] It is important to note that this definition of purpose is radically different from the neoliberal notion of maximizing shareholder wealth or profitability as the central purpose of the firm. Many observers have disagreed with that narrow purpose over the years, recognizing that businesses necessarily exist in a web of stakeholder relationships, are embedded in societies, and are deeply connected to the natural environment, which serves as the foundation of where they necessarily get their resources from. Yet the neoliberal narrative still posits this narrow vision.

Indeed, in 2000 I argued that profitability and wealth maximization are simply by-products of doing good work for some group of

---

[42]   Donaldson, T., and J.P. Walsh. 2015. "Toward a Theory of Business." *Research in Organizational Behavior* 35, pp. 181–207.

[43]   Donaldson, and Walsh, *Toward a Theory of Business*.

[44]   Donaldson, and Walsh, *Toward a Theory of Business*, 188. Caps in original.

stakeholders, treating others, for example, employees and communities, well, and creating useful products and services.[45] Later, in a book titled *Firms of Endearment: How World-Class Companies Profit from Passion and Purpose*, authors Sisodia, Wolfe, and Sheth argue much the same point based on their empirical work, which demonstrates how companies who treat their stakeholders well significantly outperform companies that do not so "love" their stakeholders.[46] Sisodia and Mackey argue similarly in *Conscious Capitalism*.[47] Sisodia with Gelb took the idea even further in *The Healing Organization*, arguing that companies that have positive impacts on people will achieve extraordinary performance.[48]

Stakeholder theorist R. Edward Freeman has stated many times in public and in writing that the idea of wealth maximization as the purpose of the firm is, fundamentally, foolish. Freeman makes the analogy that while we humans need blood to survive as companies need profits to survive, our *purpose* in life is not to make blood.[49] Similarly, companies' *purpose* is not to make money (or maximize financial wealth for shareholders) but to produce goods and services that meet needs of their stakeholders (customers), while treating other stakeholders well.

Donaldson and Walsh argue, thinking along similar lines, explicitly state that the purpose of business is the generation of collective value, defining it as "the agglomeration of the business participants' benefits, net of any aversive business outcomes."[50] While they avoid the use of the word stakeholder, these authors note that business involves a "system

---

[45] Waddock, S. 2000. *Leading Corporate Citizens: Vision, Values, Value Added.* McGraw-Hill. See also Waddock, S., and A. Rasche. *Building the Responsible Enterprise.*

[46] Sisodia, R., D. Wolfe, and J.N. Sheth. 2003. *Firms of Endearment: How World-Class Companies Profit from Passion and Purpose.* New York, NY: Pearson Prentice Hall.

[47] Mackey, J., and R. Sisodia. 2014. *Conscious Capitalism: Liberating the Heroic Spirit of Business.* Cambridge, MA: Harvard Business Review Press.

[48] Sisodia, R., and M. Gelb. 2019. *The Healing Organization: Awakening the Conscience of Business to Help Save the World.* New York: HarperCollins.

[49] Freeman, R.E. 2017. " The New Story of Business: Towards a More Responsible Capitalism." *Business and Society Review* 122, no. 3, pp. 449–65.

[50] Donaldson, and Walsh, *Toward a Theory of Business*, p. 191.

of production, exchange, and distribution relationships, among and between the entities that constitute firms' value chains: firms themselves, civil society, institutions of government, and the communities that both sustain and benefit from business activity."[51] They then define business participants as "anyone who affects or affected by business," distinctly echoing Freeman's classic definition of stakeholders, albeit broadening it somewhat to emphasize its cooperative nature, not just competition.[52]

The definition of collective value is considerably broader than traditional notions of maximizing shareholder wealth or profitability. It does include different values and benefits in what Donaldson and Walsh term an "agglomeration" of benefits, that is, a group of benefits that are clustered together but not necessarily coherently.[53] Further, these authors put limits on how businesses can operate by designating that there is what they term a dignity threshold, below which it is problematic to go. Like conflict resolution expert Donna Hicks,[54] who has written extensively on dignity and violations thereof, Donaldson and Walsh believe that all people are worthy and should be treated with dignity.[55]

In defining collective value, Donaldson and Walsh limit their understanding of collective value to business outcomes. The idea of flourishing is, however, broader. It encompasses businesses, and the collective well-being of people and their communities and institutions, as well as that of nature and all of her manifestations in the notion of responsibility for the whole—where "whole" here means the world. Collective well-being, that is, really encompasses the whole planetary system, with human systems and institutions as part of that larger system, not just how business entities make their money. Like government, business is a serious responsibility—and the systemic impacts of activity in any of these institutions need to be considered when making any business, public policy, or other decision.

---

[51] Donaldson, and Walsh, *Toward a Theory of Business*, p. 188.

[52] Donaldson, and Walsh, *Toward a Theory of Business*, p. 188; Freeman, R.E. 1984. *Strategic Management: A Stakeholder Approach*. Boston: Pitman.

[53] Donaldson, and Walsh, *Toward a Theory of Business*, p. 191.

[54] Hicks, *Dignity*.

[55] Donaldson, and Walsh, *Toward a Theory of Business*, pp. 191–192.

The very definition of what we mean by flourishing for all includes the idea of dignity, because it is impossible for people who are experiencing what Hicks calls dignity violations to experience flourishing. Dignity violations hit at the core of peoples' feelings of self-worth and affect their sense of being safe, secure, and able to function effectively in the world.[56] In other words, to experience their full functionings and capabilities, as Amartya Sen called them,[57] people need to experience dignity.

In effect, creating a flourishing world for all means adopting a new worldview, first an economic worldview, and eventually a broader one that encompasses the values articulated earlier in this chapter and deals explicitly with what it means to be human today and how we humans, as well as nonhuman beings, can lead flourishing, dignified lives. Whatever worldview eventually emerges, whether from the aftermath of the Covid-19 pandemic or through some other mechanism, it needs to be one that balances human activities with available resources and distributes them more equitably, creating the potential for all to thrive. The goal needs to be more than merely surviving, despite all the troubles facing the world. For businesses in particular, this shift will mean moving priorities away from material gain, constant growth, and financial wealth towards much more holistic conceptions of wealth and well-being, ideas that need to inform just about all decision making.

---

[56] Hicks, *Dignity*.

[57] Sen, A. 1993. "Capability and Well-Being." In *The Philosophy of Economics: An Anthology*, Daniel M. Hausman, ed. Cambridge, UK: Cambridge University Press, pp. 30–53. Also, "Well-being, Agency and Freedom: The Dewey Lectures 1984." *The Journal of Philosophy*, pp. 169–221.

CHAPTER 8

Stewardship of the Whole: Beyond Sustainability to Flourishing

If our economic and social systems are to move to purposes that emphasize relationships and give life to human and ecological systems, then significant changes are needed in businesses and other institutions. Some of those changes involve shifts in public policy in different nations to support purposes for businesses that enhance the idea of collective value for all, as we discussed in the last chapter, including flourishing ecosystems that support humanity's and other living beings' needs.

Perspectives, Power Relationships, and Practices: A Stewardship Approach

As introduced in the last chapter, what is needed today is a form of planetary stewardship—stewardship of the whole. Planetary stewardship needs to be taken up by corporate and other executives, legislators and other policymakers, and civil society in all sorts of institutions, by educators, religious and spiritual leaders, politicians, civic activists, writers, artists, and anyone else who wants to participate. Such stewardship involves finding key levers of change and generating the political will to make the necessary shifts to enhance dignity, well-being, and flourishing for all. It involves, then, all of us acting as "stewards of the future," from whatever our station, in a top-down, bottom-up, all hands on deck set of strategies to effect change towards an ecologically supportive and just world for humankind and other living beings from wherever we stand. In other words, everyone has a role to play in fostering the flourishing world we hope to bring about and overcoming the multitude of issues facing that world today.

Stewardship means holding something in trust for others, according to Peter Block, who has written the seminal management book on stewardship.[1] Stewardship invokes broad time and space scales, in caring for something that does not necessarily belong to the caretaker.[2] In a sense, being a steward of something means taking accountability for the whole entity, the system. Importantly, stewardship can involve caretaking for future beings as well as ones already present.

One group of scholars discussing "earth stewardship" argues that the Earth needs to be conceived as one global commons.[3] Just how fragile today's global commons is became evident during the Covid-19 pandemic when social and governmental institutions struggled to come up with satisfactory responses to the virus. A commons is a shared resource, like the air, water, or a flourishing natural environment. Typically, such commons have been relatively localized, but today because of the nature of the problems the world faces—pandemics, climate change, collapsing ecosystems—they are global. Earth stewardship scientists argue that humanity needs to act quickly in the interest of stewardship of the whole, to avoid a global "tragedy of the commons."[4] The tragedy of the commons is a term popularized by philosopher and ecologist Garrett Hardin that describes situations in which systems' resources are overused by some users each trying to maximize their own benefits, while disregarding (or not realizing) the impacts of the totality of their individual decisions on the whole system.[5]

---

[1]   Block, P. 2013. *Stewardship: Choosing Service Over Self-Interest* (re-issued). San Francisco: Berrett-Kohler.

[2]   Nassauer, J.I. 2011. "Care and Stewardship: From Home to Planet." *Landscape and Urban Planning* 100, no. 4, pp. 321–23.

[3]   Chapin III, F.S., S.T. Pickett, M.E. Power, R.B. Jackson, D.M. Carter and C. Duke. 2011. " Earth Stewardship: A Strategy for Social–Ecological Transformation to Reverse Planetary Degradation." *Journal of Environmental Studies and Sciences* 1, no. 1, pp. 44–53.

[4]   Garrett Hardin, G. 1968. "The Tragedy of the Commons." *Science* 162, no. 3859, pp. 1243–48.

[5]   Hardin, "The Tragedy of the Commons."

Earth stewardship is "the active shaping of trajectories of change in coupled socio-ecological systems at local-to-global scales to enhance ecosystem resilience and promote human well-being."[6] To accomplish earth stewardship, leaders, intellectuals, religious leaders, government officials, civil society actors, activists, and numerous other actors need all become stewards with an eye towards the whole system's flourishing, including all peoples and living beings, as well as preserving nonliving resources for future generations.

Earth stewardship encompasses the actions of all institutions, including business and other types of enterprises (whatever form they may take), though the scope of the stewardship is broader than that of any given enterprise. Earth stewardship involves identifying the entire planet as a global commons (hence the alternative name sometimes used, planetary stewardship). The goal of earth stewardship is to "help develop ecologically and societally sound options that enhance ecosystem resilience and human well-being."[7] In other words, Earth stewardship is about making major shifts—transformations—in what and how things are done in the world. It involves holistic understanding that engages multiple disciplines simultaneously—relationally and reciprocally—and creates new forms of social or collective dialog and decision making about how to move the whole system, at whatever level of analysis is relevant, forward.[8]

Earth stewardship fundamentally tries to link the arts, humanities, with social and physical sciences with designers and planners, leaders, and engineers, despite that these disciplines have different languages, operating styles, and even objectives.[9] Such an approach to system stewardship and transformation means acknowledging that no one approach, discipline, or type of institution has all the answers to the global challenges now posed by the need to create a world that, as the WEAll initiative says, works for all.

---

[6] Chapin et al., "Earth Stewardship." p. 45.

[7] Chapin, F.S., M.E. Power, S.T. Pickett, A. Freitag, J.A. Reynolds, J. A., R.B. Jackson, ... and A. Bartuska. 2011. "Earth Stewardship: Science for Action to Sustain the Human-Earth System." *Ecosphere* 2, no. 8, pp. 1–20.

[8] Chapin et al., "Earth Stewardship."

[9] Chapin et al., "Earth Stewardship."

Stewardship of the earth is also called planetary stewardship, defined by Seitzinger and her colleagues as the "active shaping of trajectories of change on the planet, that integrates across scales from local to global, to enhance the combined sustainability of human well-being and the planet's ecosystems and non-living resources."[10] These authors point out that because of the complexity involved planetary stewardship will be what they term polycentric, meaning governed from multiple places. Further, planetary stewardship and associated transformation efforts will need to take into consideration the "complex, multi-scalar [i.e., multiple scales or levels of analysis], and interconnected nature of today's global environmental [and other] challenges."[11] Such efforts will be "cross-scalar, multi-agent approaches,"[12] as well.

That type of complexity suggests that transformational change will result from emergent processes of interconnected initiatives, hopefully all guided by a common set of goals and objectives—new perspectives or mindsets, in fact, which Meadows points to as the most powerful lever of transformation.[13] Transformational change to be effective needs to be centered on core memes that help frame common narratives that shape policies and actions. Since it is virtually impossible to coordinate or plan transformation, by the nature of complex wickedness, or, most likely, institute governance at the planetary level in any realistic way, such narrative-based, vision-driven guidance becomes increasingly needed. That is why the idea of stewardship, particularly of the planetary future, is vitally important.

The term stewardship derives from a variety of religious traditions that seek to have humankind steward resources and valuables belonging to others. The term now crops up in many business-related initiatives, including the Forest Stewardship Council (environmentally sound forest management), the Land Stewardship Project (promotes sustainable

[10]   Seitzinger, S.P., U. Svedin, C.L. Crumley, W. Steffen, S.A. Abdullah, C. Alfsen, W.J. Broadgate, et al. 2012. "Planetary Stewardship in an Urbanizing World: Beyond City Limits." *Ambio* 41, no. 8, pp. 787–94.

[11]   Seitzinger et al., "Planetary Stewardship," p. 787.

[12]   Seitzinger et al., "Planetary Stewardship," p. 790.

[13]   Meadows, "Leverage Points."

agriculture), and the Marine Stewardship Council (sustainable fisheries). Other stewardship initiatives include the Product Stewardship Institute (reducing health, safety, and environmental impacts of consumer products), e-Stewards (e-waste management), the Alliance for Water Stewardship (promote responsible freshwater use), and the Excellence through Stewardship initiative (best practice in agricultural biotechnology).

Business associations also use the term stewardship. For example, the U.S.-based Conference Board talks about product stewardship encompassing every aspect of production, as does the chemical industry's Responsible Care initiative and CEFIC, the European Chemical Industry Council. Numerous agricultural and product-related stewardship associations exist as well, at local, regional, national, and international levels. In addition, numerous companies have adopted stewardship platforms, for example, REI (responsible business practices, connecting people to the outdoors, and protecting natural places).

A key criterion for stewardship of the whole system is that people take responsibility for something bigger than and beyond the immediate interests of their own initiative, enterprise, or company (or, importantly, self). That stewardship could revolve around the well-being of future generations of humans and other creatures that live on the home we call the earth. It could be for the capacity of the planet to support all of the living beings that exist, not just humans, and it could be for human flourishing in the context of thriving natural systems. Peter Block, for example, writes about authentic service as a core element of stewardship that exists when power is balanced, the commitment is to a larger community (versus the self), everyone is involved in defining purpose and culture, and there is balanced and equitable distribution of rewards.[14]

Earth stewardship operates on a set of core principles articulated by their framers at the Earth Stewardship Initiative. Solutions exist at multiple scales. Interactions among multiple issues (i.e., wicked problems in complex adaptive systems)[15] need to be taken into account, while aligning incentives with solutions. Change agents need to act in harmony with nature's and human communities' constraints and opportunities,

---

14   Block, *Stewardship*, Loc 273–74.

15   For example, Waddock, et al., "The Complexity of Wicked Problems."

honoring "place," while recognizing the challenges of particularly diffi-cult (and new) global issues.[16] Economic, technological, and integrative of "mosaic" approaches are all likely to be needed in the change processes, according to earth stewardship's framers.[17]

Raworth's approach to economics (often called "doughnut econom-ics") helps flesh out the roadmap to flourishing human and natural sys-tems that is at the core of this argument. Raworth combines the planetary boundaries work of the Stockholm Resilience Centre with a foundational set of 12 core human needs that set a baseline of conditions, support human beings achieving what Raworth calls an equitable and sustain-able future. Though the term flourishing seems more holistic and for-ward looking than does the term sustainable (which implies stasis or more of the same), the issues highlighted provide an excellent framework for thinking about the future.

The discussion of transformational change earlier indicates that mul-tiple initiatives, led by a wide variety of people and groups, at different levels and in many places are needed to bring about purposeful system transformation. That is why the combination of planetary boundaries and vital social foundations in Raworth's framework seem so important.

As discussed in earlier chapters, we are deeply embedded in a story of neoliberal capitalism that tells us that the sole purpose of companies is to maximize wealth for shareholders in the context of "free" markets that will supposedly solve all of society's problems. These ideas are entwined in legal understandings of the roles and purposes of businesses as well, suggesting that one arena needing significant attention will be to bring today's legal standards in line with the realities of our global ecosystems.[18] Trade among nations is also supposed to be free, responsibility is indi-vidual but not shared, and liberty or freedom to do what one wants is a paramount value. Yet as I have also tried to demonstrate, a more holistic,

---

[16]   Chapin et al., "Earth Stewardship," pp. 5–8.

[17]   Chapin et al., "Earth Stewardship," pp. 11–13.

[18]   See, for example, Capra, F., and U. Matte. 2015. *The Ecology of Law: Toward a Legal System in Tune with Nature and Community*. San Francisco: Berrett-Koehler, and Yosifon, D.G. 2013. "The Law of Corporate Purpose." *Berkeley Business Law Journal* 10, no. 2, pp. 181–230.

stewardship-based perspective is also possible, based on values of dignity and flourishing, relationship, reciprocity, responsibility, and redistribution, with principles that give life to create flourishing for all. Because business is such an important institution today, many of the changes needed begin with how businesses operate and what they are expected to do, this chapter focuses next on business transformation.

It's the System! So Act Collaboratively and Think Systemically

Companies and other organizations wanting to take a stewardship approach, even when they have visionary leaders, can find it hard to do so. In fact, in today's neoliberal economic approaches, it might even be impossible for them to do so because they (at least think they will) face competitive disadvantages in doing so—or shareholder pressures in the current system's structure. Further, there are many pressures in the system that constrain such forward-looking activities.

There is some evidence that some companies already are beginning to recognize the need to bring about systemic change, create more collaborative approaches, and work across many types of boundaries through stewardship approaches. For example, there are numerous voluntary initiatives that focus businesses on a broader set of stakeholders than shareholders and on their impacts on the natural environment have now emerged. Some financial institutions agree, among other things, to incorporate ESG (environmental, social, and governance) issues into investment decisions and analysis. Numerous other voluntary initiatives fostering corporate responsibility and even exerting some degree of pressure on businesses for better responsibility practices exist today, including some business associations that include some of the planet's leading businesses essentially ask businesses to become stewards of the future.

None of these initiatives alone is powerful enough or as yet committed to the core values articulated here to bring about needed systemic transformation, in part because they represent a more incremental, business-as-usual approach to dealing with the world's grand challenges than is needed for transformation. They do, however, represent a start at shifting the mindsets of leaders, and that start is a beginning towards the more globally systemic changes needed at the whole system level, the topic of the next chapter. Accomplishing many—if not all—of them, however, requires significant redirection and a new global mindset at the whole system level.

Practices and Policy Changes to Support Economies and Societies that Give Life

Many of these changes and others that might take place within the workplace require shifts in public opinion, followed by changes in laws and public policy to realize them in practice. One huge problem with today's system is that the very idea of "public goods" or positive externalities, has been diminished, since neoliberalism's narrative denigrates the whole idea of society and of public goods, goods like clean air and water that are shared by all. Yet the whole concept of collective value is based on the idea that public goods can (and should) be produced—and that businesses are part of that production process. Today, the externalities created by companies in this system's quest for constant material and financial growth are not generally fully counted in the costs of production, yet stewardship of the future to create a world of dignity and well-being for all demands that externalities be internalized so that businesses and their customers are aware of the full costs of production. To bring about a situation in which businesses act in harmony with nature's resources and constraints, moves in this direction—of which many are possible with the requisite political will[19]—are needed.

The discussion of collective value in Chapter 7 highlights the need for repurposing business entities, particularly corporations. Business purpose needs to be recalibrated away from an emphasis on shareholder value towards something more like collective value[20] and linkages that more closely connect companies with key stakeholders on which they are dependent—employees, customers, and communities, in particular. If they are to create collective value, then it is important to recognize that all companies, including corporations, have social purposes as well

---

[19] Political will is, of course, the major obstacle to such change.

[20] Donaldson, and Walsh, *Toward a Theory of Business.*

as economic and financial ones, and that their activities inherently affect the natural environment and all of the beings that populate it, not just human ones. To bring all of this about means making significant changes in the ecosystem that surrounds businesses—particularly the public policy context that can require new business behaviors—and, when appropriate incentives are provided, spur innovation.

Repurposing the Firm

Recognizing that all enterprises should have social purposes and impacts means going beyond common interpretations about the purposes of businesses. Too frequently today, business purpose is defined as something like maximizing shareholder wealth or making profits. Because businesses are socioecological entities, however, their impacts and hence purposes necessarily go beyond these narrow definitions. Further, today's share-oriented corporation ownership structures mean that companies have little real accountability to their purported "owners," because rather than being owned by families (or widows and children), most shares are owned by "faceless" financial institutions—who may hold the stock for limited periods of time and care mainly about financial returns rather than the public good or stakeholder, ecological, and societal benefits.

If we broaden the definition of responsibility for companies to encompass how they operationalize their business model via strategies and practices, there are a number of ways that public policies and other types of pressures can refocus how companies see their purposes and production processes. Companies in a stewardship for flourishing economy would focus on obtaining "reasonable" returns (not maximized), probably consistent from year to year rather than growth-oriented, and ensuring that in the process of making those returns they generated collective value without dignity violations.

System Change: Collective Value without Dignity Violations

Figuring out what is meant by collective value means generating new performance metrics for companies, other institutions, and societies as a whole. Collective value has the connotation of communal benefit—something that benefits the whole community, at whatever level of analysis seems relevant. Shifting away from maximized shareholder wealth towards benefiting all stakeholders while staying within the limits of the natural environment's capacity to renew, restore, regenerate, and recycle takes the principles of what gives life to systems seriously. It does, however, means a fundamental shift in the purposes of business, the mindsets or perspectives of business, governmental, and civil society leaders, and adoption of new performance metrics aimed explicitly at ensuring the good of the whole. Earlier I discussed some emerging such performance metrics, like the Genuine Progress Indicator and the OECD's Better Life Index, which make some progress along these lines. GNP, with all its flaws, is simply not the best metric for a stewardship/flourishing-oriented society.

Something more like GPI, but probably that goes beyond it, needs to be widely adopted and accepted and then businesses will be far more likely to do what is needed to achieve these new standards and meet societal expectations. As noted earlier, GPI is still framed in economic rather than fully well-being-oriented ways and that framing in a sense "buys into" the very language it is meant to avoid (which gives away the show, in a sense).[21] As is often said in accounting: you get what you measure. If what is wanted is flourishing for all, then adopting metrics that get at whether that goal is being achieved is needed. The expectation for "maximized" shareholder returns needs to be replaced by "reasonable" or "responsible" returns—enough to keep the business itself thriving without taking what economists call "rents" or excess revenues from other parts of the system (including the natural environment).

The responsibilities for companies associated with working towards a flourishing world for all include how companies produce products and supply services, what they produce, and, generally, to create a system embedded with dignity and well-being for all, where all includes the natural environment as well as the human environment. Because it is the system itself that needs to change so that businesses can also change, the following section focuses on the types of systemic pressures that businesses

---

[21] Lakoff, G. 2014. *The All New Don't Think of an Elephant!: Know Your Values and Frame the Debate*. White River Junction, VT: Chelsea Green Publishing.

face in their external environments that can ultimately pressure businesses into transformation.[22]

Emphasize Development Not Growth

The growth imperative embedded in today's dominant economic narrative is also deeply embedded throughout the economic system, which relies on constant growth in gross domestic product (GDP), company profits (and rising share prices) and market shares, as well as other indicators of continual growth for signs of health. Yet as the principles of life and Indigenous values we have discussed indicate, healthy biological and ecological systems do not continue to grow (in size) indefinitely. Indeed, there are physical limits for most biological entities, including ones that specify healthy limits, and ecological systems that are healthy increase in diversity and complexity—but not size, often because of physical constraints to growth and because healthy systems require a healthy diversity of entities to retain balance and harmony. The same is true for socioeconomic systems like communities and societies. Indeed, medical science calls uncontrolled growths cancers, yet it is to that unrealistic star of continual growth that economists have hitched their wagon.

Raworth's "doughnut" economics offers a healthier alternative to this idea of constant growth,[23] though retaining the prospect of ongoing and vibrant (alive!) businesses. While it is somewhat hard to imagine what economies or even businesses might look like without a constant need for growth in number of employees, product/service array, market share, and profitability and share price, that is the task that lies before us in moving towards flourishing for all. The approach is based on ideas about abundance, vitality, and connectedness or relationship, rather than "efficiency,"

---

[22]   I have laid out an extensive set of ideas regarding business transformation specifically in Waddock, S. 2020. "Achieving Sustainability Requires Systemic Business Transformation." *Global Sustainability*, URL: https://doi.org/10.1017/sus2020.9 (accessed May 4, 2020). Some of the material in this chapter draws from and builds on what is written in this paper.

[23]   Raworth, K. 2017. *Doughnut Economics: Seven Ways to Think Like a 21st-Century Economist*. White River Junction, VT: Chelsea Green Publishing.

exploitation, and extraction. Imagine businesses actually creating collective value. They would serve their many stakeholders in a variety of dignity-enhancing ways that include sustainable and productive employment for many people, providing decent wages and job security, collaborating with a variety of stakeholders in local and global communities, and internalizing the many externalities of their operations to achieve full costing of products and services.

Focus on Employment and Job Production

The world in the future is in serious need, not of more productivity and efficiency (though for ecological reasons, both remain important), but of more jobs or decent work for all capable people with greater redundancy and resilience. Equitably paid jobs can ensure that more people can obtain what the International Labor Organization calls "decent work" and earn living wages that support their families. Work also provides meaning for many people, because it enables them to achieve a dignified status of supporting themselves and their loved ones, and because when embedded in purposeful enterprises, work itself can be meaningful. The principle of redistribution from Indigenous thinking suggests that such jobs' pay needs to be equitable in reasonable proportion to what, for example, chief executives make, avoiding the inequities so present in today's system.

Universal Basic Income

In a desirable transformation, companies would be measured not only on how much productivity they have achieved, though that will undoubtedly remain important, but also on how many jobs they create and sustain over time, and the equity in their salary structures. Stable local employment also improves communities because the local populace has money to spend, local businesses are supported, taxes are paid, and the community can afford to provide needed services like education and infrastructure. These lessons became apparent even before the Covid-19 pandemic, when conversations about providing something like universal basic income for everyone began to gain prominence. A universal basic income would guarantee that everyone has enough to live on, whether they are working or not, and assure a certain level of dignity for all.[24] Even more powerful, as David Korten argues, would be for individuals to be able to participate in a regenerative process of engagement in working with the very resources on which they depend.[25]

Pay Equitable Decent Wages and Provide Job Security

Except in cases where employees are irresponsible, unproductive, or otherwise problematic, measures of company performance in a stewardship future may well assess the extent to which a company's employment is stable, plus whether compensation is equitable, fair, and provides a living wage for all employees, not just top management. These factors are essential to jobs that provide dignity and flourishing. In addition, turnover and retention indicators will be important proxies for employee well-being in areas where there are plentiful jobs to be had. Further, organization cultures that make work life enjoyable, productive, and fulfilling rather than simply tolerable (or necessary) can enhance dignity for participants. In global supply chains, such indicators are even more important in light of all the issues associated with working conditions in developing nations and will receive even more scrutiny than domestic working conditions.

Collaborate and Compete

Another of the memes that drives much company behavior today is the assumption that it is competition that produces good performance—and that companies are independent actors, somehow separated both from society and nature. Yet biologists and ecologists would be among the first to note that nature itself is not truly based in "nature red in tooth and claw" as the poet Tennyson described it. Rather, nature operates with a healthy combination of symbiosis—or collaboration—and competition.

---

[24] Gentilini, U., M. Grosh, J. Rigolini and R. Yemtsov. 2019. "Overview: Exploring Universal Basic Income." *World Bank eLibrary* URL: https://elibrary. worldbank.org/doi/full/10.1596/978-1-4648-1458-7_ov (accessed February 6, 2020).

[25] David Korten, personal communication.

Indeed, nature, like Indigenous wisdom, suggests that symbiosis (reciprocity) is the core value, with some competition but most reliance on cooperation. Thus, both collaboration and competition are necessary in successful ecosystems, including business ecosystems. This idea is reflective of Michael Porter's work on successful economic clusters, that is, groups of companies in an industry whose activities are related to and networked with each other. The health of clusters, replete with diverse enterprises, connections, purposive organizing, continual innovation, viewed holistically, illustrates clearly the need for collaborative as well as competitive strategies.[26]

Companies stewarding the future can expect to experience significant new demands for partnership, not just with other firms, but with entities from other sectors as well, particularly around the grand challenges facing all of us, many of which are articulated in Raworth's doughnut model. Some competition for resources is, of course, necessary, but equally, if not more important, are the collaborative efforts of entities working holistically together in relationships and with reciprocity and responsibility for the whole towards a healthy ecosystem—whether that is a business, societal, or natural ecosystem. The key to healthy, flourishing in ecosystems of all sorts, and a key for thinking about stewardship, is requisite diversity—entities of all sorts and biodiversity—in creating the system resilience, adaptiveness, and transformability necessary for healthy ecosystems.[27]

Since the 1990s, companies have been joining with actors in other sectors to form cross- or multisector collaborations of various kinds and this activity has only picked up in recent years. A stewardship future will very likely involve numerous such coalitions, including coalitions of business leaders like the World Business Council for Sustainable Development and the World Economic Forum that deal with the issues of sustainability—in its broadest definition of sustaining the natural environment, the business, and the community. Coalitions allow participants to engage

---

[26]   Porter, M.E. 1998. " Clusters and the New Economics of Competition." *Harvard Business Review 76*, no. 6, pp. 77–90.

[27]   Folke, C., S.R. Carpenter, B. Walker, M. Scheffer, T. Chapin, and J. Rockström. 2010. "Resilience Thinking: Integrating Resilience, Adaptability and Transformability." *Ecology and Society* 15, no. 4.

with and learn from each other to create the innovative approaches and solutions to issues that are demanded in difficult times, but that no one entity can achieve by itself because of the complexity and wickedness of the systems involved.

Develop and Use Energy Wisely

In a stewardship future, massive shifts in the nature and type of energy that businesses and other enterprises (as well as individuals) use will be needed to reduce carbon emissions and deal with some of the negative impacts of climate change. A shift towards energy that is renewable will diminish the use (abuse, some might say) of fossil fuels (coal, oil, gas). Fossil fuels have numerous negative eco-impacts. Using renewable and nonpolluting energy sources, including solar, wind, geothermal, water-powered, hydrogen, and other sources of energy that do not demand or damage nearly as many eco-re-sources as today's power sources do, is a huge need. That shift is, in many respects, already underway as companies, governments, and individuals begin to respond to the imperatives posed by climate change. Certainly, the shutdown of economies during the Covid-19 outbreak dramatically demon-strated that pollution is far less problematic when fewer fossil fuels are used.

Innovate in Line with Nature's Constraints

The nature of innovation itself changes in a stewardship future. For exam-ple, in producing products companies need to foster regenerative inno-vations that use renewable resources to replace nonrenewables, reuse old resources, restore systems that are outdated with new ones—through soft-ware, not hardware, and regenerate natural systems rather than exploiting them. They can emphasize innovative design processes like biomimicry,[28] or designing products, materials, and systems based on biological princi-ples.[29] When natural resources do inevitably need to be used, companies would need to provide for the renewal and restoration of those resources

---

[28] Benyus, J.M. 1997. *Biomimicry*. New York, NY: William Morrow.

[29] For examples, insights, and ideas, see the Biomimicry Institute website, https://biomimicry.org/ (accessed May 27, 2020)

in a variety of innovative ways—and in a timeframe consistent with nature's. From a sustainability perspective, companies will simultaneously have to ensure that any renewable resource that is used is replenished, and that such resources are not drawn down beyond their replacement rate.

Those demands are consistent with The Natural Step's four principles approach to sustainability. Collectively, they should foster increased innovation as companies work—and innovate, doing what companies do best—to meet these demands. The Natural Step argues that "In a sustainable society, nature is not subject to systematically increasing:

- Concentrations of substances from the earth's crust (such as fossil CO_2, heavy metals and minerals);
- Concentrations of substances produced by society (such as antibiotics and endocrine disruptors);
- Degradation by physical means (such as deforestation and draining of groundwater tables);
- And in that society there are no structural obstacles to people's health, influence, competence, impartiality and meaning."[30]

The key to implementation, of course, is that the system around companies, which places these demands on them, needs to shift so that all companies are subject to similar sets of dynamics and constraints, fostering a healthy set of innovation and competitive pressures.

Produce Quality Products/Services that Meet Real Needs

Far too many products produced today need to be "marketed" to unwary customers, who already have far too much "stuff." Particularly in highly industrialized nations, there is a lot of product saturation and less natural demand for new products than might otherwise be the case. As a result, highly sophisticated (and sometimes somewhat deceptive) marketing practices are too often used to sell sometimes unnecessary goods and services to customers, creating new markets where no natural markets

---

[30] The Natural Step, "Four basic rules define success: We call these rules 'Sustainability Principles.'" URL: https://thenaturalstep.org/approach/ (accessed April 24, 2020).

exist. Systemically, this excess production creates significant waste of both produced goods and the materials and resources used in the production, often for goods used only once or a few times and then discarded.

This approach to selling goods and services, frequently described as a "take-make-waste" approach,[31] needs to shift radically to bring businesses into accord with both nature's constraints and humanity's real needs. If collective value were defined as doing good for the community, then companies could sometimes produce and sell products or services that are actually needed but that might not be as profitable as some other products and services. For example, clean water in developing nations, low-cost, low-resource use sanitation facilities, and healthful food products, may be somewhat less profitable (or are viewed as not being as profitable because production is more difficult in some places), so companies avoid making them. Yet, there are real needs in the world demanding to be met—and there are, in fact, profits to be made if the incentive is to create collective value rather than simply generate maximized profits.

Businesses with a stewardship mindset, intent on meeting broader purposes of job creation and sustainability, resource use reduction, renewal, and restoration, would be willing to make less profit for serving the public good if they were reputationally rewarded for serving collective value. Further, innovative firms can find significant opportunity in meeting real needs. Holistically, such an approach to creating products and services that meet real needs, rather than manufactured ones, can enhance dignity and flourishing for all in many ways, through the provision of new jobs, by creating goods and services that people really want and need, and generally enhancing life for customers and the societies in which they live. This approach ties in with the need to shift company purposes towards more holistic goals of flourishing and dignity.

Create Product/Service Standards of Quality, Durability, and Renewability

In line with making reasonable financial returns while service the purpose of collective value, renewed emphasis on product durability, quality, and

---

[31] McDonough and Braungart, *Cradle to Cradle*.

longevity in the stewardship system would replace the use-a-few-times-and-throw-away or "throw-away society" mentality that currently exists. The days of planned obsolescence, instituted to create new markets in the 1950s and continued to this day, need to be replaced by an emphasis on product durability and quality, and presumably accordingly higher prices. Despite higher prices and costs of production, durable, quality products that last longer and quality services should be more valuable to customers, who in a holistic approach to stewardship would have the resources to afford such quality. Holistically, for example, if people have stable, decent paying jobs, they will be able to afford higher quality products and services, including public services and goods like clean air, water, education, and good infrastructure.

Durable, high-quality physical products and infrastructure, however, means that people individually will need fewer things and they will be replaced less frequently. Again systemically, quality and durability create a need for higher levels of craftsmanship, higher quality raw materials, and, hopefully, less waste in the production process. From a systemic perspective, this approach, then, can potentially create needed new and meaningful work for many people. Of course, excellent education, apprenticeships, and ongoing training activities will also need to be systemically incorporated into a whole system geared at producing quality projects that meet real needs.

Servicizing and Software Updates, Not Constant New Products

The idea of servicizing is that companies sell services rather than physical products. Servicizing is also a potentially important business model in a stewardship economy, where durability and quality, rather than constant product churn, are emphasized.[32] Servicizing as outlined by thought leader Allen White simply means that the company provides the service that a customer desires, for example, refrigeration rather than refrigerators, or transportation rather than vehicles. While products are still required in such an approach, the company retains ownership, creating even more

---

[32] White, A.L., M. Stoughton, and L. Feng. 1999. "Servicizing: The Quiet Transition to Extended Product Responsibility." *Tellus Institute, Boston* 97, pp. 1–89.

incentives for the company to produce high-quality, durable, and service-able products rather than ones that need replacement every few months. The benefit for the company is that there is a kind of retainer or fee paid for the service over the long term, so companies using this approach can create a sustainable long-term business model.

Some countries including Germany already have "take-back" laws that reinforce this type of approach. In a take-back approach, the company retains responsibility for the disposal and hopefully recycling of large items, like washers and dryers, or electronics that might otherwise be thrown into the garbage. While take-back laws emphasize waste management, they also create incentives for companies to produce higher quality goods so that they do not need to be returned and recycled often.

A similar approach is useful for products embedded with software. Software updates and improvements to existing products could conceivably replace hardware updates on many products. That would prevent replacing an electronic device simply because it looked outdated or because some new features were available on newer models. In the churn mentality, companies want to sell new phones, creating huge piles of digital equipment waste. In a stewardship approach, they will take responsibility for creating a durable product that can be upgraded periodically. Customers who desire upgrades should be willing to pay for them, especially if there are not always "new models" available with different features, creating a sound business model for companies supplying the upgrades. Then the physical products would only be replaced when they are truly no longer usable. If they are built to easily be recycled, and are both durable and of high quality, then significant waste reductions can occur. In short, the entire system needs to be reoriented towards longevity of hard and soft goods, including clothing and other consumer products, rather than product churn.

Shift Power: Internalize Externalities, Externalize Public Goods

In economic thinking, an externality is a side effect of the production process or of doing business that is not reflected in the costs of production of the relevant goods and services or the prices paid by customers. Externalities can be positive at times, for example, the availability of well-educated workers in a community with a strong educational system or the pollination services delivered by bees otherwise being kept for their production of honey, things that actually add value overall to the system. Such positive externalities are typically called public goods.

Many so-called externalities, however, are destructive or negative. Such negative externalities are of most concern in today's system, as we consider how to transform it towards well-being and dignity for all. Such externalities reduce the overall value in the broader system, but are not taken into account in the costs associated with their production. Pollution from manufacturing affects waterways, lakes, and oceans. Trash created by disposable plastics and other detritus of our throw-away culture now circulate in vast oceanic swirls. Fertilizers and pesticides that aim to keep mono-cultural agricultural practices productive run-off into streams, lakes, rivers, and ocean. Animals kept penned up in their own waste are fed antibiotics that create drug resistance in bacteria to prevent illnesses caused by their housing and close quarters. All of these things, along with many others, represent negative externalities. Air pollution from fossil fuels from both vehicles and manufacturing processes, water pollution from various effluents, and even noise pollution represent other forms of negative externalities.

In addition, the true costs of negative externalities, not to mention the full costs of production, remain unincorporated into the prices of goods and services, since legal accounting practices enable companies to avoid internalizing costs now externalized. In other words, companies are not taking into account the full costs of their products and services from a social and ecological perspective. Externalization, however, does not mean that the costs go away, for they remain somewhere in the system. Sometimes those costs are borne by taxpayers, who have to pay for pollution cleanup. Other times they are borne by people who suffer ill effects physically from the externality. Many times, poorer people suffer more from externalities than do wealthier people, because the latter are able to find ways to avoid the costs. Creating systemic flourishing means finding new ways to deal with these costs so that they are either not created in the first place or are fully incorporated into the prices of goods and services. Further, these shifts need to happen without diminishing the capacity of all people to access truly needed goods and services, thereby reducing the costs of inequality.

Internalized Costs and Integrated Reporting

In line with internalized ecological and social costs that are now external-ized would require a globally coordinated effort by governments around laws and regulations on reporting practices, by audit and accounting firms, including firms who assess environmental, social, and governance (ESG) considerations, and by multilateral entities like the UN to change auditing and reporting practices. The model for such change already exists, albeit in the context of voluntary ESG reporting, with the evo-lution of the Global Reporting Initiative (GRI) as the global standard for such reporting. What needs to happen globally is that this type of reporting be mandated—and that companies are regularly assessed for their performance on relevant indicators as they contribute to collective value (and avoid dignity violations).

Several countries already require that listed companies report on "material" ESG risks and expenditures, and more significant changes can be expected within the next few years. South Africa requires listed firms to produce not just ESG reports, but integrated reports. This requirement actually preceded the formal release of integrated reporting framework in late 2013 by the International Integrated Reporting Council (IIRC).[33] With the Integrated Reporting (<IR>) framework now seen as a key framework for tackling climate change by accounting organizations glob-ally,[34] <IR> is only likely to gain more traction in coming years. Compa-nies of any size can expect that within the foreseeable future, they will all be expected to produce integrated reports, which are assumed to foster more integrated thinking about the impacts and costs associated with company performance.

---

[33] Integrated Reporting (<IR>) website. Home (2020). https://integratedreport-ing.org/, (accessed, April 24, 2020).

[34] Integrated Reporting (<IR>) (2020. International <IR> framework recom-mended as a key framework in call for action by A4S and accounting bodies internationally to tackle climate change. Integrated Reporting website, https://integratedreporting.org/news/international-framework-recommended-as-a-key-framework-in-call-to-action-by-a4s-and-accounting-bodies-internationally-to-tackle-climate-change/ (accessed April 24, 2020).

<IR>, as noted by the framework document, fosters integrated thinking that helps organizations understand the interdependencies and trade-offs surrounding the various capitals that are necessary for success (see also, Waddock, 2002). <IR> also is expected to enhance the ability to respond to legitimate stakeholder interests. It can shape how organizations develop strategies and business models with respect to the external environment. It can also help the organization monitor its performance holistically and with a past, present, and future orientation. Notably, all of these elements are necessary underpinnings of the stewardship of the future that I am describing as the core role for tomorrow's companies.

Foster Long-Termism

Some companies are already trying to think longer-term, by resisting issuing "quarterly earnings guidance," that is, reports to analysts about what to expect in the next quarter. Even the venerable McKinsey Consulting Company has argued that such earnings guidance was "misguided," creating greater share price volatility without actually doing much to reflect earnings that annual reporting did not do, and indeed that there were "real costs" associated with issuing such guidance without much benefit.[35] *CFO Magazine* suggests that such guidance may be necessary in "red flag" situations to give a warning to investors and analysts that something may be wrong. Otherwise it seems to agree with the McKinsey paper,[36] and among others, the CFA Institute and Business Roundtable have called on managers to stop issuing such guidance earnings in the interest of fostering a longer-term orientation.[37]

---

[35] Hsieh, P., T. Koller and S.R. Rajan. 2006. "The Misguided Practice of Earnings Guidance." *McKinsey on Finance* 19, pp. 1–5.

[36] Baham, R. 2012. Letting go of guidance. *CFO Magazine* (November 12, 2012). http://ww2.cfo.com/forecasting/2012/11/letting-go-of-guidance/ (accessed August 29, 2018)

[37] Dean Krehmeyer, Matthew Orsagh and Kurt N. Schacht, Kurt N. (2006). Breaking the short-term cycle. CFA Institute (2006), URL: https://www.cfainstitute.org/-/media/documents/article/position-paper/breaking-the-short-term-cycle.ashx, (accessed August 29, 2018).

The business-led environmental organization Ceres similarly calls for "ending the tyranny of short-termism" by fostering "capitalism for the long term."[38] Even high-profile economist Michael Porter with Mark Kramer has called for companies to create "shared value."[39] Porter and Kramer further argue that the "capitalist system is under siege" and likely to remain so without significant changes towards a different understanding of how businesses serve—or steward—societal interests.[40] All of these initiatives begin to move companies away from short-term profits and growth towards longer term performance with different kinds of benefits and are necessary systemic shifts towards transformation to a world of flourishing for all.

Flourishing and Life Not Growth

There are, of course, many other systemic changes that would foster new innovations and transformation in the business community, while still allowing businesses themselves to thrive—and the system itself to move towards flourishing based on principles that give life and take responsibility for the whole system—as the Indigenous wisdom discussed earlier articulates. The ones above are offered to help reframe some of today's ideas towards business in the direction of flourishing for all—and the creation of collective value. In the next chapter, we will continue this exploration, focusing on values that shape whole society perspectives (and, in turn, business ones), and continuing to build on the principles outlined by Indigenous wisdom and what gives life to systems.

---

[38]   Dominic Barton, " Capitalism for the long term," *Harvard Business Review* 89, no. 3, pp. 84–91.
[39]   Porter, M.E., and M.R. Kramer. 2011. "Creating Shared Value." *Harvard Business Review* 89, nos. 1/2, pp. 62–77.
[40]   Porter and Kramer, "Creating Shared Value." p. 62.

CHAPTER 9

New Economies Oriented towards Life

Shifting towards a mindset that encompasses dignity, equity, and flourishing for all means thinking on a whole system—indeed, planetary—scale. It is not just one sector, for example, business as discussed in the last chapter, that needs to change. All major socioeconomic and socioecological systems need reorientation towards flourishing and away from growth-at-all costs and financial wealth as the ultimate goals—and towards socioeconomic system considerably more life—and relationship-oriented. That shift needs to happen globally, though obviously in culturally and context-sensitive ways. It cannot be done by the colonizing people, nature-dominating mindset that has characterized the industrial era—or even the Enlightenment. It needs to be done through what Andreas Weber calls "Enlivenment"[1] by adopting an Enlivenment mindset that puts the connectedness (relationships) and life discussed in the last few chapters first.

As made evident during the isolation and economic devastation, many people experienced during the Covid-19 pandemic, there are human values more important than monetary wealth. These values connect us with each other and with what ultimately matters in a more transcendental sense. That is what the Indigenous values and life-giving principles tell us.

From a planetary perspective, the earth system as a whole has constraints related to the number of human beings (and other critters) the planet can support flourishing for all. Nature trades in abundance—but it is abundance in variety or diversity and connections, not continual growth.[2] There are also constraints on how much of earth's resources can

---

[1] Weber, Enlivenment.

[2] Weber, Enlivenment.

be used for any given generation or population. Ecologists John Ehrenfeld and Andrew Hoffman put the need very succinctly, saying that human beings and businesses in particular "have to wake up the fact that *more is not better!*"[3] Perhaps the Covid-19 crisis has brought the opportunity for just this awakening but only if, as ecologists say, we can build back better, not "bounce back" to the system causing so many problems.[4]

Societal changes at the whole system level are needed. Indeed, *society* needs to change so that businesses can change, because businesses are embedded in societies and operate under the set of constraints and pressures imposed by those societies' norms, expectations, regulations, and laws. Most businesses cannot change on their own because of systemic pressures and constraints that hold current operating practices and mindsets in place.[5]

Thinking about transformation towards a more equitable, flourishing world is particularly important in the years following Covid-19 and on into the future. Here is a striking reality: The old system is unlikely to return to its former state however much some people might like it to do so—and even though many of us hunger for a return to business as usual. The nature of complexly wicked systems will prevent that because too much will have changed in the time between when the pandemic started and when it ends—if it ends.

Both complexity and wickedness exhibit path dependencies, which means that once a change has started, it is impossible to return to the original state. Just think of the businesses and restaurants that will never reopen, or that will have changed how they operate to accommodate the crisis. Or think of how learning and teaching will likely change because so many instructors have had to put lessons on line. Think, indeed, of how

---

[3]   Ehrenfeld, J., and A. Hoffman. 2013. *Flourishing: A Frank Conversation about Sustainability*. Palo Alto: Stanford University Press.

[4]   At this writing, I am working with two different initiatives using these types of concepts. WEAll, the Wellbeing Economy Alliance, is using the phrase "bounce back better" and the SDG Transformations Forum is creating an initiative called "bounce beyond" with the idea that simply bouncing back to the same old/same old system is going in the wrong direction.

[5]   See Waddock, "Achieving Sustainability."

many parents will value teachers more after trying to educate their own children at home—and while working. Think of how many people will have learned how to work from home. Think of the long-term economic devastation that will be wrought by the pandemic on individuals who have been unemployed or laid off or whose jobs have simply disappeared. Think of the people who will have been lost to the virus—whose lives have been cut short and the emotional wreckage those losses for their loved ones. Things simply will not and cannot return to the way they were. Too much has been, is being at this writing, lost or permanently changed.

The key, then, is to find ways to motivate the change that is actually needed now—transformation towards what enhances relationships and supports life and flourishing for all, including greater equity, dignity, and connectedness with self, others, and nature.

The old story of constant growth to attain material/financial wealth needs to be seen in the more realistic light of the limitations that exist on how far planetary resources can be pushed before ecosystem (or societal) collapse ensues. Never before in the geologically relatively short span of human history has humanity had the capacity—as it now seems in the era or the Anthropocene to have—to create systemic collapse at a planetary level. That potentiality is made more poignant by the realization from anthropologist Jared Diamond that the two main causes of systemic collapse are pushing beyond ecological limits and growing inequality,[6] both of which the world as a whole faces today if significant changes are not put in place in the relative near term.

Indeed, ecologist Tim Jackson argues for ending what he calls the myth of decoupling. Relative decoupling is what Jackson says is the unrealistic idea that production and consumption patterns and processes can be sufficiently redesigned that the planet can support all of humankind more equitably. What Jackson calls absolute decoupling means significantly decreasing overall consumption or what some people call "degrowth," despite that vast swaths of the human population that currently exist at or below the poverty level—making that magnitude of change in resource

---

[6] Diamond, J. 2005. *Collapse: How Societies Choose to Fail or Succeed*. New York: Penguin.

use an unlikely prospect.[7] Interestingly, during the shutdown accompanying the pandemic, skies cleared, pollution diminished, "shopping" slowed dramatically, airline travel nearly ceased, and many other changes that move towards a healthier ecology took place even while social systems were put under massive strain.

Some observers, including Richard Heinberg of the Post Carbon Institute, believe that "Economic growth as we know it is over and done with."[8] Many initiatives are already working to shift towards what "new economies," built around the types of principles discussed in this book. At least until the pandemic hit, however, powerful vested interests kept the business-as-usual system in place, despite the existential threat posed by climate change—and are likely to try to return the system as much as possible to its former state.

Depressing as these insights might be, they are reinforced by the findings of the Intergovernmental Panel on Climate Change (IPCC) regarding the risks associated with climate change.[9] They are supported by other scientists who have highlighted what they term a planetary emergency deriving from climate change.[10] The Covid-19 pandemic has brought these existing and highly problematic issues into clear relief. The crisis, however, may have also opened up many people's mindsets—perspectives—to new possibilities, new ways of thinking—new paradigms and mindsets supported by reframed cultural mythologies that support flourishing for all. Whatever we might believe about the feasibility of reimagining and redesigning the world to support all of life, including all of humanity, I believe that hope and optimism that such transformation is possible is necessary to motivate action. Thus, the rest of this chapter focuses on outlining some ideas that give shape to life—and relationship-centric economy.

---

[7]   Jackson, T. 2011. *Prosperity without Growth: Economics for a Finite Planet.* Abington, UK: Routledge.

[8]   Heinberg, R. 2011. *The End of Growth.* New Society Publishers, Loc 180.

[9]   IPCC. 2014.

[10]   Ripple, W.J., C. Wolf, T.M. Newsom, P. Barnard, W.R. Moomaw and 11258 others. 2019. "World Scientists' Warning of a Climate Emergency." *Bioscience* https://academic.oup.com/bioscience/advance-article/doi/10.1093/biosci/biz088/5610806?searchresult=1 (accessed April 13, 2020).

Practices and Power: Operating Principles Shaping Life-Giving Perspectives and Practices

The discussion below builds on the principles and values discussed in the last chapter, that is, relationship/connectedness, responsibility, reciprocity, redistribution, purpose, diversity, boundedness, novelty, and wholeness. There are obviously many different ways such principles might be expressed and built into socioeconomic systems, so the rest of the chapter will explore some of the ones that seem to have the most leverage for true systemic transformation.

Circularity

The principle of circularity, often conveyed by the term circular economy, encompasses a number of important ideas to support a holistic, reciprocal, interconnected, and diverse understanding of the system. Writing to distinguish between concepts of sustainability and circular economy, Geissdoerfer, Savaget, and Bocken[11] point out that the term circular economy encompasses multiple other sustainability-oriented ideas, including a cradle-to-cradle economy,[12] regenerative capitalism,[13] closed loop economy,[14] and biomimicry,[15] among others. The MacArthur Foundation provides a definition of a circular economy as "an industrial economy that is restorative or regenerative by intention and design,"[16] picking up on several related concepts. The MacArthur definition continues: "It replaces the 'end-of-life' concept with restoration, shifts toward the use

---

[11] Geissdoerfer, M., P. Savaget, N.M. Bocken and E.J. Hultink, E.J. 2017. "The Circular Economy—A New Sustainability Paradigm?." *Journal of Cleaner Production* 143, pp. 757–68.

[12] McDonough and Braungart, *Cradle to Cradle.*

[13] See, for example, Fullerton, Regenerative Capitalism.

[14] Stahal, W.R. 2016. " Circular Economy." *Nature*, pp. 435–38.

[15] Benyus, *Biomimicry.*

[16] MacArthur, E. 2013. "Foundation. Towards the Circular Economy: Economic and Business Rationale for an Accelerated Transition." *MacArthur Foundation*, p. 7. https://werktrends.nl/app/uploads/2015/06/Rapport_McKinsey-Towards_ A_Circular_Economy.pdf

of renewable energy, eliminates the use of toxic chemicals, which impair reuse, and aims for the elimination of waste through a superior design of materials, products, systems, and within this, business model."[17]

Circularity also differentiates between durable goods and "consumable" ones, made of materials that decay and actually do become "food" for another part of the system without creating toxicity in the process. When durable goods are needed, according to the MacArthur Foundation's conception, they are built to last and need to be designed for reuse, restoration, and renewal rather than being simply discarded. As the MacArthur Foundation notes, a circular or regenerative economy "designs out waste" moving towards what McDonough and Braungart called "cradle-to-cradle" design in which "waste equals food." That is, what is waste for one part of the system becomes food (or input) for another part.[18] The third principle MacArthur Foundation articulated was that of what was earlier identified as "servicizing"[19] or converting "consumers" into "users" who lease or rent products for the services they provide rather than purchasing and then discarding them.

Such an approach changes economic thinking considerably because it inherently incorporates what are now considered externalities into design and manufacturing processes, ensuring their full costing. As Stahel put it, a circular economy "would change economic logic because it replaces production with sufficiency: reuse what you can, recycle what cannot be reused, repair what is broken, remanufacture what cannot be repaired."[20] From the perspective of the system as a whole, the movement in circularity incorporates ideas of reciprocity, responsibility for the whole system, and stewardship of all resources over long periods of time, much as the Indigenous thinking explored in the last chapter argues for.

Interestingly, circularity as a foundational economic principle also has a great potential to generate innovation, though it would be innovation aimed at enhancing durability and quality of products (and services to some extent), figuring out how to renew, reuse, and recycle resources, and fostering ever-greater efficiency through resource stewardship. Companies

---

[17] MacArthur Foundation. "Towards the Circular Economy." p. 7.

[18] McDonoug, and Braungart, *Cradle-to-Cradle*.

[19] White et al., "Servicizing."

[20] Stahal, " Circular Economym." p. 435.

in a circular economy would build reputations for the quality, durability, flexibility, and re-usability of their goods, would avoid product churn and excessive marketing, and would engage in creative designs that worked to really meet, as opposed to manufacturing, people's needs.

Think "Enough!" Not More

If there is one word that might describe the underlying philosophy of neoliberalism it is the word "more." The whole idea of "enough" or sufficiency counters that idea of ever-more stuff or wealth. The concept of enough can mean having reached some sort of limit in which more would be excess or, more minimally, that some sort of basic threshold has been reached. As Laura Spengler argues, both of these conceptions can be combined to reflect the core idea embedded in thinking about ecological sustainability.[21] In a world facing limits imposed by the overuse of resources, fostering an "enough" mindset might be a helpful way to achieve sustainability, while still allowing for the abundance and diversity of flourishing to occur in nature. Of course, as Spengler notes, there is debate about whether "enough" should be viewed as a minimum or maximum, especially around moral issues like equity or what is needed to live a good life.

Some theorists believe that sufficiency or enough is a moral minimum for values like distributive justice, so that, at minimum, people's basic needs are met.[22] At the same time, some environmentalists believe that enough/sufficiency should be treated as a maximum, in that some people have "enough stuff" and should modify lifestyles to bring them into better alignment with nature's constraints.[23] Alexander has called an approach to "enough" at the societal level, a "sufficiency economy," arguing that the "growth paradigm has no future."[24] The core definition given is that "the

---

[21]   Spengler, L. 2016. "Two Types of 'Enough': Sufficiency as Minimum and Maximum." *Environmental Politics* 25, no. 5, pp. 921–940.

[22]   Spengler, L. "Two types of 'enough'." p. 925.

[23]   Spengler, L. " Two types of 'enough'." p. 925.

[24]   Alexander, S. 2012. "The Sufficiency Economy: Envisioning a Prosperous Way Down" https://ssrn.com/abstract=2210170 or http://dx.doi.org/10.2139/ssrn.2210170 (accessed November 13, 2012).

sufficiency economy aims for a world in which everyone's basic needs are modestly but sufficiently met, in an ecologically sustainable, highly local-ized, and socially equitable manner."[25] As argued earlier, such a perspective would shift economies away from the growth-at-all-costs model towards a more balanced, living-in-harmony with nature approach, consisted with both the principles that give life and Indigenous values discussed in the last chapter.

Alexander's notion of a sufficiency economy builds on several prin-ciples that may begin to sound familiar. The goal, as he articulates it is, "Enough for everyone, forever," with the fundamental idea that econ-omies should not seek growth but rather a standard of living that per-mits all participants to live decently,[26] encompassing values of reciprocity, responsibility, and redistribution. Using the principle of diversity, he further argues that after the basic standard of living is achieved, any "growth" is not in size or material goods. Rather what emerges is diversity or abundance of renewed relationships with other people and nature in communities, meaningful work, creativity, and spiritual practice. These characteristics reflect what is envisioned in the Indigenous values and principles that give life to socioeconomic systems discussed earlier. In other words, communities and people having their basic needs met, as with universal income for all, would be free to engage in other pursuits (novelty) that they find meaningful, whether through engaging with oth-ers, being creative, practicing spirituality, growing gardens, exhibiting their creativity, helping and caring for others, being connected to nature, or in other ways.

Live Big and Think Small

Big is not always better. In a nongrowth-oriented economy, company sizes, market share, and growth rates may well be limited to what can adequately be managed at a local level—and to sizes that serve the needs within a given, probably local, market, an approach that might be called

---

25   Alexander, "The Sufficiency Economy," p. 2.
26   Alexander, "The Sufficiency Economy," p. 9.

being in right relationship to the context and set of needs.[27] Ironically, reducing the scale and scope of businesses (and other entities as well) may be key to fostering healthier human and natural systems—and system resilience. Not only do smaller scale entities have small impacts both socially and ecologically, but they also have the potential to create more jobs, more innovations, and less resource-intensive products and services. That is, they generate more systemic resilience, helping to solidify their identity (boundedness) and sense of purpose because they are connected to system participants in meaningful ways. Under these circumstances, there is considerably more diversity in types and kinds of businesses and hence a natural resilience emerges along with a sense of abundance along the lines that healthy ecosystems provide.

To avoid the problem of lack of resilience, big companies could also divest unrelated businesses and allow "many flowers" or businesses to bloom independently. In doing so, they will avoid "growth" strategies that simply mean acquisition of formerly independent companies to make them appear bigger and more dominant in their markets. New bases of competition will be likely to be durability, quality, and service—reputational assets that gain the trust of a variety of stakeholders including customers, employees, communities, suppliers and distributors, and governments.

There is considerable evidence that "right sizing" things, not in the sense of making companies smaller so they can lay off employees and shave expenses, but in the sense that there seem to be reasonable and workable sizes for communities, companies, and other institutions so that they do not become unwieldy and rigid. Such right-sized (bounded and whole within themselves) entities would not be "too big to fail" as the saying went about big financial institutions during the Global Financial Crisis of 2007–2008. "Right-sized" institutions of all sorts exhibit not only more resilience and adaptability, but also more diversity, which as

---

[27]   David Korten has long been an advocate of such thinking. See, for example, David, K. 2010. *Agenda for a New Economy: From Phantom Wealth to Real Wealth*, 2nd edition. San Francisco: Berrett-Koehler, and Korten, D. 2015. *Change the Story, Change the Future: A Living Economy for a Living Earth*. San Francisco: Berrett-Koehler Publishers.

discussed is a sign of a healthy ecosystem, whether ecological, business, or community.

Right-sized communities too can enable participants in the system to be explicitly more connected with each other because the size of the system is not overwhelming. These ideas also apply to interconnected businesses and industries. Economist Michael Porter recognized the truth of this idea in developing his notion of successful business clusters, in which a diverse array of different types of businesses "fed" each other or "served" others, creating healthy industrial clusters.[28]

Stay Local and Build Healthy Communities

The idea of enough or sufficiency, discussed above, is related to ideas about localization, both for businesses and communities—albeit in a context in which globalization is also likely to continue. Local and smaller businesses are better interconnected to and with participants in their communities and in a sense pressured to operate more responsibly (responsibility, connectedness) than are huge essentially rootless companies with few local ties. Businesses in a new economy system could be evaluated for their (positive or negative) impacts on local community life in places where they operate, that is, the extent to which they foster greater or lesser community stability, well-being, and quality of life[29] or what Donaldson and Walsh call collective value,[30] as discussed earlier.

Developing nations will be far more likely to be open to trade and creating business opportunities in a more equitable world, where their own people are not simply exploited for the purpose of satisfying consumers in the developed world (novelty, wholeness, redistribution, and responsibility). But the nature of trade is likely to change to much more of a

---

[28]   Porter, M.E. 1998. "Clusters and the New Economics of Competition." *Harvard Business Review*, 76, no. 6, pp. 77–90, and Porter, M.E. 2000. "Location, Competition, and Economic Development: Local Clusters in a Global Economy." *Economic Development Quarterly* 14, no. 1, pp. 15–34.

[29]   See Korten. Fall 2017. *Agenda for a New*. Also David Korten, "Ecological Civilization and the New Enlightenment." *Tikkun* 16–23, p. 70.

[30]   Donaldson, and Walsh, *Toward a Theory of Business*.

self-sufficiency model than the current exploitive model that drains local resources away from developing nations, if nations and their communities were to rediscover their own, culturally appropriate ways of doing things rather than relying on a fragile, ecologically expensive, and exploitative global system. The same ecological limits and constraints made obvious by the pandemic make clear that ideas about equity and social justice demand a very different understanding of "economy" in the future than has been present since neoliberalism gained dominance (responsibility, reciprocity, connectedness).

New and Renewed Forms of Business

Consider, for a moment, the global financial crisis of 2007–2008. It was created in part because the financial system is now intricately linked into a web of dependencies that rely on a few—not very diverse or resilient—mega-financial institutions and huge monolithic corporations. The economic system at the global level is comprised of huge institutions, including businesses, with enormous (and highly interdependent) supply and distribution chains comprised of much smaller enterprises. Indeed, in August 2018, it was announced that for the first time one company's (Apple Computer) total market value topped $1 trillion. While there are millions of small and medium-sized enterprises (SMEs), it is the oligopolies and near monopolies that now exist in many industries, overall that capture much attention. Collectively, these mega-corporations created a system that lacks the diversity, connectedness to other stakeholders, sense of broader purpose, or capacity for innovation (novelty) associated with healthy ecosystems, not to mention good businesses, all of which are fundamental principles of life-giving economic and social systems.

Given these realities of large enterprise, it is increasingly clear that the global economic system needs to incorporate resilience and diversity, so that adaptability and "transformability," the capacity to transition to the next stage when needed, can be improved. Biodiversity is the key to resilience ecologically. Big, as noted, is not always better in ecological terms. Many big companies, including airlines, retail firms, the travel industry, giant industrial agriculture firms, and manufacturing firms found themselves in significant trouble during the Covid-19 pandemic in 2020.

That is because they lacked resilience and because they had stripped so much "slack" from their systems in the interests of purported efficiency and financial growth that they lacked adaptive capacity when pressured. The same holds true for human systems.[31] Of course, many small businesses, which do not have the (theoretical, if not in practice) slack that larger companies have, always found themselves at great risk of not being able to reopen after a crisis as well.

Scholar Gerald Davis has pointed out dramatic shifts both in the nature of corporations since the 1960s and in their number, shifts he attributes to the dominance of finance and shareholder-oriented capitalism[32]—or neoliberalism as termed here. As companies globalized, they shifted manufacturing operations overseas to smaller suppliers and created globally connected supply chains, moving manufacturing away from wherever headquarters companies were located, often to locations with few social and ecological regulations—in the interests of "efficiency." From 1988 through 2008 (when the Global Financial Crisis hit), the number of companies listed on the U.S. stock exchange dropped dramatically from a peak of nearly 9,000 in the mid-1990s to just fewer than 4,500 in 2008.[33] These shifts, according to Davis, are related to the "financialization" of the economy which has, in his view, "maimed" society[34] for many of the reasons discussed throughout this book, including the constant attention to share price rather than business fundamentals.

Davis further shows that the vast majority of companies in the Dow Jones Industrial average for 1973 were manufacturing and consumer goods companies. That mix of firms had shifted dramatically. In 1962, he

---

[31] Something that Schumacher pointed out in long ago, Schumacher, E.F. 1973. *Small is Beautiful: A Study of Economics as if People Really Mattered.* London: Blond and Briggs.

[32] Davis, G.F. 2013. " After the Corporation." *Politics and Society* 41, no. 2, pp. 283–308.

[33] Davis, "After the corporation," p. 291.

[34] Davis, G.F. 2009. *Managed by the Markets: How Finance Re-Shaped America.* New York: Oxford University Press; Davis, G.F. August 2010. "The Rise and Fall of Finance and the End of the Society of Organizations." *Academy of Management Perspectives* 23, no. 3, pp. 27–44; Davis, G.F. 2010. "Not Just A Mortgage Crisis: How Finance Maimed Society." *Strategic Organization* 8, no. 1, pp. 75–82.

points out that the top five companies in terms of market capitalization (total market value) were AT&T, General Motors, Exxon, DuPont, and IBM. By 2012 that mix had become Apple, Exxon, Microsoft, Google, and Walmart—with Exxon the only industrial firm left, and the others either technology firms or retailers.[35] In 2020, the United States' largest five companies by market capitalization were Microsoft, Apple, Amazon, Alphabet (Google's parent company), and Facebook—all of which are high-tech firms that create an environment that Shoshana Zuboff has called "surveillance capitalism." What Zuboff means is that some of the big tech players take (use without their knowledge or permission) people's private data from them and use it to help boost profits for these and other companies.[36]

Gerald Davis asks an important question addressed in the next section: can an economy survive without corporations?[37] And answers it in the affirmative. There is a lot more sympathy from communities for smaller, local, and more diverse forms of enterprise than for large multinational corporations—whether industrial, retail, or high-technology firms. Small firms are necessarily sensitive to local concerns and community needs, for the simple reason that they are rooted locally and their leaders and employees need to face community members on a daily basis. Davis further notes that though the proportion of large, shareholder-owned, megalithic, and market-dominating corporations is shrinking and their life spans also decreasing but that what is left in their wake are the inequalities, ecological catastrophes, shrunken governments, and other dysfunctionalities discussed throughout this book.[38] That leads to the next discussion about alternative ways of organizing that might be

---

[35]   Davis, G.F. 2016. "Can an Economy Survive Without Corporations? Technology and Robust Organizational Alternatives." *Academy of Management Perspectives* 30, no. 2, pp. 129–40.

[36]   Zuboff, S. 2019. *The Age of Surveillance Capitalism: The Fight for a Human Future at the New Frontier of Power*. London: Profile Books.

[37]   Davis, "Can an Economy Survive Without Corporations?"

[38]   See Davis, G.F. 2016. *The Vanishing American Corporation: Navigating the Hazards of the New Economy*. San Francisco: Berrett-Koehler; Davis, G.F. 2010. "Twilight of the Berle and Means Corporation." *Seattle UL Rev.* 34, p. 112; Davis, G.F. 2013. " After the Corporation." *Politics and Society* 41, no. 2, pp. 283–308.

more life-enhancing than the corporate form that legal scholar Joel Bakan called pathological by design.[39]

Power and Participation: Alternative Ways of Organizing

Recognition that all enterprise is social—that businesses are necessarily embedded within societies, which in turn are necessarily embedded in the natural environment—has created a good deal of interest in new business forms. Not all businesses are corporations; certainly not all are large multinationals, and even their number appears to be shrinking as noted above. The World Bank Group estimated in 2013 that there were as many as 365–445 million micro-, small, and medium-sized enterprises (SMEs) in the world. Of this estimate, some 25–36 million entities were formal SMEs, 55–70 million were formal micro enterprises, and the vast majority, 285–356 million are informal enterprises.[40] The World Bank also noted in 2020 that "formal" SMEs make up about 90 percent of total businesses and employ about 50 percent of workers, and that those numbers increase substantially when the informal sector is included. Further, formal SMEs contribute greatly to their societies, particularly in emerging economies, with as much as 60 percent of total employment and 40 percent of national incomes, and 7 of 10 jobs, attributed to these smaller businesses.[41]

Because they are smaller, SMEs' ecological impacts tend to be less than those of large corporations. Because they are locally known, SME owners have to pay more careful attention to a variety of stakeholders

---

[39] Bakan, J. 2004. *The Corporation: The Pathological Pursuit of Profit and Power*. New York: Free Press.

[40] Stein, P., O. Pinar Ardic, and M. Hommes. 2013. "Closing the Credit Gap for Formal and Informal Micro, Small, and Medium Enterprises." *The World Bank*, http://documents.worldbank.org/curated/en/804871468140039172/pdf/9491 10WP0Box380p0Report0FinalLatest.pdf?ref=hackernoon.com, (accessed April 28, 2020).

[41] The World Bank. 2020. "Small and Medium Enterprises (SMEs) (Finance)." *The World Bank Website* (2020). https://worldbank.org/en/topic/smefinance (accessed April 28, 2020).

than do large multinationals, which tend not to identify with any particular place or groups of stakeholders. Creating a flourishing future means reemphasizing and focusing on such smaller, locally rooted enterprises that emphasize community[42] (relationships, reciprocity, responsibility) and in so doing generating the kind of collective value oriented towards the good of the whole system discussed earlier.

The number and types of hybrid organizations that are alternatives to traditional corporations are growing. Some of these businesses explicitly highlight the social and ecological aspects of their purposes. New business forms include B-Corporations, "benefit" corporations, CICs (in the UK, formed for community benefit), and L3Cs (started in Vermont, formed for charitable or educational purposes).[43] Such entities, sometimes called social enterprises, are explicitly dual—or multipurpose, often stakeholder-oriented companies. At least in theory they use the power of business to solve social and environmental problems while also making (reasonable) profits.

B-Corporations, for example, enable companies to go beyond so-called constituency statutes, by explicitly developing multiple bottom lines. Constituency statutes, which at least 34 states in the United States now have passed,[44] permit companies to pay attention to business-related stakeholders other than shareholders. They do not, however, necessarily permit explicit attention to human rights, racism, nature, or global issues such as poverty,[45] although increasingly activists are calling on companies to tackle these issues, too. As of 2020, more than 3,300 (mostly small

---

[42]   Korten, D. 2018 "From the Theory of the Firm to a Theory of the Community." *Living Economies Forum* http://davidkorten.org/theory-firm-theory-community/ (accessed April 28, 2020).

[43]   Reiser, D.B. 2011. "Benefit Corporations-A Sustainable Form of Organization." *Wake Forest Law Review* 46, pp. 591–625.

[44]   Dizikes, P. 2016. "Laws Allowing Companies to Prioritize Stakeholders Boost Innovative Activity." (*Phys.Org,*) February 17, 2016, URL: https://phys.org/news/2016-02-laws-companies-prioritize-stakeholders-boost.html (accessed April 28, 2020).

[45]   Munch, S. 2012. "Improving the Benefit Corporation: How Traditional Governance Mechanisms can Enhance The Innovative New Business Form." *Northwestern Journal of Law and Social Policy* 7, pp. 170–95.

or medium-sized) companies in 150 industries and in 71 countries have voluntarily become certified as B-Corporations.[46] The B-Corporation movement recognizes that "Society's most challenging problems cannot be solved by governments and nonprofits alone." Therefore, businesses need to be engaged as well in issues like poverty and inequality reduction, creating conditions for a flourishing natural environment, and creating jobs with dignity and purpose.[47]

B-Corporations are explicit about their stakeholder commitments, and submit themselves to social auditing and explicit stakeholder responsibilities and interest is growing.[48] Companies that wish to become B-Corporations need to be certified through B Impact Assessments that determine how the company's strategies, operations, and practices impact a wide range of stakeholders associated with the firm.[49]

In its "Declaration of Interdependence," B-Corporation envisions "a global economy that uses business as a force for good," through purpose-driven companies that create "benefits for all stakeholders, not just shareholders."[50] B-Corporation has created B Lab as a nonprofit to serve the interests of creating a global movement around B-Corporations, fostering more B-Corp Certifications, and otherwise promoting the idea of businesses as a force for good. B Lab works with related types of organizations like Benefit Corporations that "join the interests of business with those of society," attempting to influence their emergence globally. A benefit corporation is a for-profit corporation in the United States, at this writing authorized by 36 (with five more working on legislation) U.S. states and the District of Columbia that deliberately includes positive societal, worker, community, and ecological impact in its mission, as well as profitability.

---

[46] B Corporation. 2020. "B Corporation (2020)." URL: https://bcorporation. net/about-b-corps, (accessed April, 28, 2020).

[47] B Corporation, Certified B Corporation.

[48] Munch, " Improving the Benefit Corporation."

[49] B Corporation. 2020. "Certification" URL: https://bcorporation.net/certification

[50] B Corporation. 2020. "About B Corps" URL: https://bcorporation.net/ about-b-corps (accessed April 29, 2020).

Additionally, there are numerous hybrid organizations formed around dual-bottom-line purposes, often called social enterprises. Collectively, these entities are part of what some call an emerging fourth sector,[51] which combine the social interests of the NGO with the business orientation of the firm. The late-20th and early 21st centuries also witnessed the emergence of many new forms of cross-sector social interactions, including public–private partnership, multisector alliances, and stakeholder networks. Accompanied by a general blurring of sector and organizational boundaries,[52] such entities represent grassroots forms of change of the sort that Schumpeter called creative destruction.[53]

Initiatives, even movements, aimed at reforming capitalism itself are cropping up to these changes and especially public interest in seeing change. For example, Conscious Capitalism, spearheaded by then Whole Foods CEO John Mackey and scholar Raj Sisodia, focuses on four key principles for businesses. Its human-centric capitalism emphasizes that companies need meaningful purpose beyond money and profits; conscious leadership that focuses on "we" rather than "me," a stakeholder orientation that encompasses shareholders and includes all who contribute to a well-functioning business; and "conscious culture" or embedded values, principles, and practices that shape the social fabric of a business.[54] Another project is called Inclusive Capitalism. This global effort attempts to engage leaders in business, government, and civil society in efforts to make capitalism more equitable, sustainable and inclusive, and hence more prosperous long-term benefits.[55]

All these innovations are potentially fruitful and necessary; however, none provide the necessary leverage for true system change to deal with

---

[51] Sabeti, H. 2010. "The For-Benefit Enterprise." *Harvard Business Review* 89, no. 11, pp. 98–104. See also Fourth Sector.net, "About the Fourth Sector" 2020. https://fourthsector.net/the-emerging-fourth-sector (accessed April 29, 2020).

[52] Crane, A., and M.M. Seitanidi, eds. 2014. *Social Partnerships and Responsible Business: A Research Handbook*. Abington, UK: Routledge.

[53] Schumacher, E.R. 2011. *Small is Beautiful: A Study of Economics As If People Mattered*. New York: Random House.

[54] Mackey, J., R. Sisodia and B. George. 2013. *Conscious Capitalism: Liberating the Heroic Spirit of Business*. Cambridge, MA: Harvard Business Press.

[55] Inclusive Capitalism. 2018. https://inc-cap.com/ (accessed April 29, 2020).

the major issues noted above. Ironically, the pandemic combined with growing awareness of the disastrous potential of climate change might provide just such a platform, assuming the right initiatives could come together and influence policy makers, civil society leaders, and businesses. All enterprises no matter what their size are embedded within the larger contexts of the communities and societies in which they operate. That embeddedness means they all have social and ecological impacts, even when their ecological footprint is reasonable. This core recognition that all enterprises, including corporations, are social—and are *part* of the broader socio-political-economic and ecological landscapes is a central element of thinking for any form of collective value—and life-centered economy in which flourishing for all is the central purpose.

Organizing to Leverage a Flourishing Future

For transformative change for such a system to develop, key leverage points need to be tapped that shift the priorities and dynamics of doing business in the world, as Meadows reminds us.[56] What matters from this perspective is *what* the impacts are—are they work that provides meaning and dignity, jobs that provide income and security, and community and national rootedness that provide a needed tax base to support necessary infrastructure, educational systems, and other services, products and services that customers, or, really, citizens truly need and value? Or are they something else altogether? Below are some possible ways to create such positive leverage by thinking about forms of organizing other than the corporation—which some have called pathological because of its orientation towards profitability and growth at all costs.[57] In addition, most of these alternative forms provide far greater organizational democracy and participation for employees—voice—something that is vital to creating life-enhancing enterprises than do corporate forms.

A form of enterprise that can work more effectively to provide a different kind of balance between stakeholder interests and the natural

---

[56]   Meadows, Leverage Points.
[57]   Bakan, J. 2004. *The Corporation: The Pathological Pursuit of Profit and Power.* New York, NY: Free Press.

environment than do corporations is that of the cooperative (coop or co-op). According to the International Labor Organization, a cooperative is an independent association of individuals "united voluntarily to meet their common economic, social, and cultural needs and aspirations through a jointly owned and democratically controlled enterprise."[58] In some cases, cooperatives can enhance the ability of otherwise marginalized people to participate actively in and learn through enterprises where they actually have a clear stake in the well-being of the enterprise and in its operations. According to the International Cooperative Alliance, cooperatives include more than a billion people globally, sustaining employment for up to 12 percent of the employed in G20 nations. They contribute some $2.6 trillion to the global economy, with claims that up to one in six people in the world are affiliated with at least one cooperative.[59] Approximately 279 million people are employed in or in the scope of cooperatives—more than 9 percent of the employed population globally.[60]

Cooperative forms provide an alternative to the traditional corporation, and it is one premised on a set of core values articulated by globally agreed principles. These principles place fairness and equality at the core, with goals of building a better world through cooperation. Principles for cooperatives include being owned and run by members, who have an equal say in how the business operates and share in profits (including customers, employees, and residents).[61] Cooperatives are considered more democratic, community, and stakeholder-friendly than are corporations because they emphasize values of "self-help, self-responsibility,

[58]   International Labor Organization. 2020. "Co-operatives" https://ilo.org/global/topics/cooperatives/lang--en/index.htm (accessed April 29, 2020).

[59]   International Cooperative Alliance. 2020. "Co-operatives" https:// ilo.org/global/topics/cooperatives/lang--en/index.htm (accessed April 29, 2020).

[60]   Hyung-sik Eum. 2017. "Cooperatives and Employment, Second Global Report, 2017." http://cicopa.coop/wp-content/uploads/2018/01/Cooperatives-and-Employment-Second-Global-Report-2017.pdf (accessed April 29, 2020).

[61]   International Cooperative Alliances. 2020. "Cooperative Identify Values and Principles." https://ica.coop/en/whats-co-op/co-operative-identity-values-principles?_ga=2.248343361.734938683.1533575354-1607872645.1533575354 (accessed April 29, 2020).

democracy, equality, equity and solidarity."[62] The world's biggest cooperatives at this writing were France's Crédit Agricole Group (about $104 billion) and Group Caisse E'Epargne ($58 billion) (banking/credit unions), and Japan's Zen-Noh (National Federation of Agricultural Cooperatives) (nearly $57 billion) followed by France's Confederation National du Credit Mutel (nearly $57 billion).[63] These statistics indicate that the cooperative form, which is rooted in its stakeholders' interests and their communities, is far from a trivial way of organizing.

Another organizing form (in the United States, mostly) is the ESOP, employee stock ownership plan, companies in which companies implement a program that ensures that employees obtain shares of the company to ensure that they take an owners' orientation to the well-being of the firm and its stakeholders. Unlike coops, however, ownership is not necessarily evenly distributed, nor are actual voting rights on company decisions accorded to all of the shareholders. Ownership by employees can be partial, with relatively less democratic voice for employees, or majority (or, occasionally 100 percent) owned. Distribution of rights can be dependent on employment tenure, with such approaches sometimes used to prevent hostile takeovers of the firm. An estimate from the National Center for Employee Ownership indicated that as of 2019 some 6,600 ESOPs exist that cover more than 14 million employees.[64] Benefits to employees in ESOPs include higher wages and better retirement assets, and, in some cases, more voice in decision making in the firm.[65]

---

[62]   International Labor Organization. 2018. "Cooperatives." http://ilo. org/global/topics/cooperatives/publications/WCMS_496599/lang--en/ index.htm. See also International Cooperative Alliance. 2020. "Cooperative Identity, Values and Principles." International Co-operative Alliance. https://ica.coop/en/whats-co-op/co-operative-identity-values-principles?_ga=2.248343361.734938683.1533575354-1607872645.1533575354 (accessed April 29, 2020)

[63]   The Guardian. CA. 2020. "The World's Biggest 300 Co-Operatives." https:// theguardian.com/social-enterprise-network/2012/jan/04/social-enterprise-blog-co-operatives-and-mutuals (accessed April 29, 2020)

[64]   National Center for Employee Ownership, "ESOP (Employee Stock Ownership Plan) Facts." 2020. NCEO, https://esop.org/ (accessed April 29, 2020).

[65]   National Center for Employee Ownership, ESOP.

Some companies use open book management to help improve results and better engage employees in understanding how the company runs. Such an approach means that the company's accounting is transparent to employees, who can then better figure out how to improve operations. The idea behind open book management is that more knowledgeable employees will be more engaged with their work and with the company's business operations—and help make improvements.[66] Key principles of open book management include continuous learning, ownership of the firm's activities, delegation of responsibilities, inclusiveness, and better teamwork, among others.

In nations like China, some companies take the form of state-owned enterprises (SOEs), that is, companies created by governments for commercial purposes. The Organisation for Economic Co-operation and Development (OECD) defines an SOE as any corporate entity recognized by national law as an enterprise, and in which the state exercise ownership.[67] Ownership by the state (government) can be complete or partial, with specific types of business purpose sometimes identified. The OECD stresses that the general public is the "ultimate owners of state-owned enterprises,"[68] bringing some (at least theoretical) degree of accountability to them. In the United States, mortgage companies Fannie Mae and Freddie Mac, and the postal service are considered to be SOEs, while Eskom, a power utility, in South Africa is state-owned.[69]

---

[66]   Stack, J., and B.O. Burlinham. 2003. "A Stake in the Outcome." https://altfeldinc.com/pdfs/stake.pdf, based on *A Stake in the Outcome: Building a Culture of Ownership for the Long Term Success of Your Business*. New York: Random House.

[67]   OECD. 2018. "Ownership and Governance of State-Owned Enterprises: A Compendium of National Practices." OECD, URL: http://oecd.org/corporate/Ownership-and-Governance-of-State-Owned-Enterprises-A-Compendium-of-National-Practices.pdf (accessed April 29, 2020).

[68]   OECD. 2018. "Ownership and Governance of State-Owned Enterprises: A Compendium of National Practices." OECD URL: http://oecd.org/corporate/Ownership-and-Governance-of-State-Owned-Enterprises-A-Compendium-of-National-Practices.pdf (accessed April 29, 2020) p. 15.

[69]   Investopedia. 2018. "State-owned enterprise—SOE" https://investopedia.com/terms/s/soe.asp

SOEs can sometimes benefit from financial support from their government through low-interest loans, or other favorable tax policies, as well as potentially a large customer base.[70] On the disadvantage side, SOEs can be subject to strong government restrictions and control, little employee voice or democracy, and strong political influence, among other possible disadvantages.[71]

Towards Life

It is the capacity for more people to be democratically engaged in these types of enterprises—more power and more voice—that gives them potential to be part of a life-affirming socioeconomic system. All of these changes will require changing status symbols away from "more stuff" towards "enough stuff," with the fundamental question no longer being, "How can I get more?" but rather "How much is enough?" These types of shifts require very different perspectives (mindsets) and purposes than have been dominant, returning not to "good old days" that never really existed, but to a reimagined future in which values about what really matters to people take precedence. What really matters, made evidence, and apparent during the pandemic are family, friends, community, belonging, social justice, and equity—or fairness in the system, honesty and truth, and the ability to live a dignified life.

---

[70] Cant, R. 2013. "Advantages and Disadvantages of Selling to Chinese State-Owned Enterprises." *Global Tax Blog* , URL: https://kahnlitwin.com/blogs/tax-blog/advantages-and-disadvantages-of-selling-to-chinese-state-owned-enterprises (accessed April 29, 2020).

[71] Cant, "Advantages and Disadvantages."

CHAPTER 10

So What? What's Next? What Can You Do?

Indigenous values of relationship, responsibility, reciprocity, and redistribution (relational values for short), combined with values that give life (purpose, connectedness, diversity, boundedness, novelty, and wholeness), I have argued, need to be central in emerging socioeconomic thinking, language, and action. While this proposition is radically different from today's dominant economic thinking, it is based in long-standing knowings, long-valued ways human beings have interacted with the world—knowings and ways that, as the physician's oath goes, do no harm, or at least mitigate the deadly harms that the world is currently experiencing.

Covid-19 is only one manifestation of a world in trouble. More ecologically threatening—existentially threatening—potential exists in the human-induced climate emergency and sustainability issues discussed earlier. More socially threatening is the inequality that caused so many protests to erupt around the world in 2019 and early 2020—only to be magnified even more by the pandemic's shattering of the illusion that the world could continue on business as usual.

Without further colonizing already colonized Indigenous peoples and, hopefully with their grace and help, all of humans need to embed both Indigenous relational wisdom and life-enhancing principles firmly into institutional (and personal/community) purposes, perspective, performance metrics, and, ultimately practices and power relationships that shape a future life-centric socioeconomic system. These Indigenous and life-affirming values intersect in important ways to create new—yet ancient and time-tested—ways to think about humans' relationships (connectedness) to each other and nature. They can also shape how societies need to transform to cope with the aftermath of the pandemic as well as the existential risks posed by climate change and social dysfunction that were already threatening the world's socioeconomic systems.

Some Questions to Frame Your Own Transformation Work

Collectively, we all need to do our bit to generate (and regenerate) a flourishing future for all, and I do mean all. Bringing about this transformation will be difficult—but hopefully is doable. Indeed, the European Union at this writing is already forwarding a new policy plan called a European Green Deal. In the United States, a Green New Deal (at this writing stalled) has also been put forth. Both would help a good deal. The Covid-19 pandemic may well—if enlightened policy makers act—push the type of new/old ideas discussed throughout this book into play, helping to content with both the pandemic and the climate emergency that is becoming increasingly urgent.[1]

Regenerative communities, cities and whole countries adopting Raworth's Doughnut Economics, transition towns and cities, regenerative agriculture, farming, and capitalism, approaches to systemic finance, and many other initiatives are shaping and guiding the many pathways to transformation. But it will take action by all of us, each in our own ways, to make transformation a reality.

If we take relational and life-affirming principles/values seriously, then depending on own talents, preferences, and instincts, and considering where each of us might have some influence on a relevant system, there is much that can be done. This brief chapter outlines some of the ways in which any of us—you!—might connect with others working to bring about system change—whether locally in our communities, schools, churches, businesses, and governmental bodies, more at a provincial or

---

[1] Hepburn, C., O'Callaghan, B., N. Stern, J. Stiglitz, and D. Zenghelis. 2020. "Will Covid-19 Fiscal Recovery Packages Accelerate or Retard Progress on Climate Change?" Oxford Smith School of Enterprise and the Environment, Working Paper No. 20-02, https://smithschool.ox.ac.uk/publications/wpapers/workingpaper20-02.pdf (accessed May 5, 2020).

state level, nationally, or even globally. We each have unique gifts. The key is for you to find and use the ones available to you.

With your indulgence, I would like to address you, the reader, directly in this short conclusion to challenge you to think about *how* you might think about becoming part of the necessary transformation towards a world of flourishing for all. To think about how you might act to bring transformation about, I believe you might want to consider some of the questions below may be helpful—for yourself as no one can or should force you to do anything that does not make sense to you.

What Is the Scope of Your Interest and Influence?

One thing to determine is what is the scope of your interest and potential influence? Do you want to work primarily at the local or community level—influencing where you live and how things work there? Do you want to work at the community, urban, state, or regional level? Is your scope somehow integrated with the type of work you do, potentially influencing an organization of some sort and how it operates? Are you interested in working to change things at a national or even global level? What types of networks or organizations do you belong to that are working on aspects of system transformation? Are they primarily local, community-based, regional, national, or global? Are they political, environmental, artistic, social, or civic? Where might you fit into their work?

What Story Are You Telling about the World?

Throughout this book, I have argued that system transformation starts with the narrative or the story we understand and tell about how the world works and what our place is in that world. What story are you telling about the world? What story do you want to tell? Can you use the ideas—the memes—of relationship and life discussed in the last few chapters—to frame new stories and narratives, new ideas and insights, rather than constantly falling back into the old ones that are so common? The idea that we are all connected, for example, is powerful—we are all part of this world, including being part of nature, and what we do in the world matters if we recognize those connections. What conversations are

you having where you could inject some of these—or your own transformational—ideas? What kind of world do you want to live in—and what
kind of world do you want your children and grandchildren to live in?
How can you help bring that world into being?

Changing mindsets—a key step in transformation—starts with the
stories and narratives we tell, the conversations we have, the words,
images, phrases, and ideas we put forward (that is, the memes). It is up
to each of us to counter the old stories (of disconnection, individualism, purportedly free markets, and the like) in whatever ways we can.
We can offer new stories in conversations, in writing, through art, or
by sharing interesting pieces with new perspectives with our friends and
acquaintances in a variety of ways. Who can you share your new stories with—around the dinner table or at the pub? In your social circles,
work environment, spiritual gatherings, community organizations, and
elsewhere? In teaching whatever it is you teach—with your children or
grandchildren? In the movies and shows you choose to watch and discuss
over dinner or at the breakfast table? At the knitting group, over a glass
of wine or beer, around a car that is being repaired, or wherever good
conversations happen.

What Issues and Domains of Activity Interest You Most?

Some people are interested in politics, others in particular issues like the
natural environment, social justice, climate change, saving whales, shifting agricultural practices, forest restoration, changing the purpose of the
corporation, or any number of the other issues that are associated with system transformation. Some are interested in improving education, either in
specific geographies or at different levels. Others are interested in working
to create more stakeholder-friendly or ecological responsible businesses.
Still others emphasize different forms of activism around issues that form
the social core in Raworth's doughnut framework. Some people work to
inform legislators and other governmental actors (locally, at the state/pro-
vide level, nationally, globally) about new ideas, raise issues, or suggest
changes needed. There are any number of possible domains of action that
might interest you. Which issues and domains intrigue you? Which would
pull you into action? Where can you get involved in those issues?

What Are the Skills and Talents You Can/Want to Bring to Bear on Transformation?

Maybe you have a particular talent or set of skills that could pull you into transformation activities. Some people are really good at using social media, for example, to broadcast ideas like the ones associated with relationship and life-giving principle and values. Others are networkers and coalition builders. Some are teachers or health care providers. Some are artists and storytellers, comedians, or activists. Others can write, for example, op-eds to the local newspaper or for publications with a broader reach. Some people may be able to create videos about these ideas to post online in a variety of places to begin to shift the conversation. During the pandemic, it was interesting to see that people with very different skill sets stepped up action in a variety of ways—cooking healthful meals and sharing knowledge about that, sewing masks and other protective gear, teaching others how to exercise at home, repairing things that broke, doing gardening, and any number of other things.

Are you an artist of some sort? Could you create and disseminate your art with the new memes in mind, so that it tells a new yet ancient story about humanity and a flourishing world, or gets people questioning the old story in some way? Many times artists are "seers" in that they have a vision of the future that differs from the common understanding and is forward-looking. Can you use your art to put forward this new vision in a song, a painting, sketch or drawing, a poem, a quilt, a piece of woodcraft, a sculpture, a short story, a novel, an essay or blog, a video, a collage, or some sort of installation—or any other art form that appeals to you? Art often reshapes how others think. Art is an important aspect of changing the story or narrative and thereby shifting mindsets towards a new, flourishing world perspective.

What Networks Are You Part of to Build New Narratives or Coalitions for Action?

Are you part of networks that could and would be able to spread new ideas about flourishing for all widely, influencing opinion/thought, organizational, and political/governmental leaders to adopt them—and ultimately build them into policy decisions? Who can you pressure to achieve needed reforms and how? What action groups are already working towards the ends that you particularly see as desirable—and how can you join with them?

What Social or Conventional Media Can Expand the Influence of Ideas about a Flourishing World for All?

Social media—platforms like Facebook, Twitter, Instagram, LinkedIn, and innumerable other outlets—can greatly amplify messaging. If you have a new story to tell, action to generate, network to solidify, initiative to organize, or collaboration to develop, how can you use social media to amplify and extend your messaging? Might you, for example, use your Facebook connections to share some new ideas and gently prod people's thinking towards a transformed and flourishing world for all? Can you learn how to make ideas "go viral" on social media—and greatly increase the number of people who see and ultimately use them? Can you become an Internet guru or knowledge maker in a realm where you have expertise and knowledge? Is that what interests you?

Can You Work on Transformation through Your Work?

Where is your paid work accomplished if you work outside the home? Can you influence thinking in that context? Where do you have the opportunity to share your version of the new story—a story about relationship and connection, what gives life to systems, responsibilities both individual and collective, about working collaboratively and in connected ways, with others? Can you bring, for example, a healthy stakeholder perspective to the work environment, to your enterprise (where that term is used broadly for any type of organization that accomplishes work of some sort)? Can you incite a renewed respect for nature and an unwillingness to exploit her resources further? Can you exert this influence upward in the enterprise, downward, or laterally? All are important. What allies and coalitions for change can you build and deploy when new decisions are made that might shift how the enterprise operates.

What Can You Do as a Citizen Activist?

There are things that anyone can do—as citizens and activists, as leaders of businesses, and of course as policymakers—to bring about system transformation. Write public officials. Join groups working for change. Build community-based organizations. Write letters to the local newspapers or write a blog and post it into social media or send it to the local newspaper. Make a piece of art that speaks about what a new economy looks like. Sign petitions that seek things like a Green New Deal. Or, well, as must be obvious by now, specific action is up to each individual's preferences and abilities.

One thing is clear. It will take political "will," combined with the desire to make positive change in the direction of flourishing for all. Generating political will requires both pressuring and educating policymakers at all levels and all places. It takes activism and upward pressure from citizens on current power players. It takes a mindset shift that empowers each of us directly to act, from whatever perch we have. Transformation is not about expecting that leaders—who are mostly already benefiting from the current system—will magically change their minds or come to see the "light," such as it is. It is about exerting leverage on the system, wherever appropriate and possible to bring about needed changes. It is about social, civic, artistic, and political action at a fundamental level and from many, many people each with unique "stories" to tell in unique ways.

The core argument I have been making is that there needs to be a pivot or towards thinking about economies and societies as whole systems that give purpose, meaning, connection/relationship and life to their inhabitants, including all people—not just an elite few—and to nonhuman inhabitants as well. Achieving that transformation means co-creating the mindsets, structures, and infrastructure to support life and relationship rather than simply gearing everything towards the accumulation of ever-more financial wealth. Continual economic, financial, and material "growth" is simply not an option. All of this means adopting and implementing new values along the lines of the relational and life-affirming values discussed earlier, all aimed at pushing the world towards flourishing for all, really for all!

Importantly, financial wealth, in the end, is empty and meaningless, as ironically enough, Covid-19 bluntly and dramatically demonstrated. If nothing else, the economic shutdowns and sequestering demonstrated for many people the importance of relationships with family and friends, the value of healthy communities, and the need for governments that work in the best interests of their people rather than the selfish interests of leaders. It highlighted inequities in the system—and the need for greater equity going forward. In the United States in particular, the pandemic pointed out the failures of the health care system and the problems that arise when leaders think too narrowly about their own interests rather than whole system needs. It also highlighted the very human need to be out in and connected with nature, when for many people the only way to be out of their homes during the crisis was to go outside for a walk or other exercise—safely, of course.[2]

Ironically, the Covid-19 pandemic also demonstrated the absolutely-essential work of people whose work is sometimes not valued much at all—the ones who help connect us to each other, to our future, and to the very food and supplies that are needed to live. Teachers come to mind, for as many parents struggled to work from home while simultaneously attempting to school their children, they began (finally some might say) to realize the valuable services that teachers provide—not to mention their skill at actually getting young children to learn. The virus also highlighted the essential foundational work done by farmers, growers, and harvesters, and others in the food supply chains—the people who actually produce, harvest, prepare, and deliver the food that we eat. It brought forward the now seen as essential delivery people and employees in stores who keep shelves stocked and food available for purchase in stores and pharmacies. And the mailpersons who deliver the mail, and the workers who deliver packages ordered online. And the workers in pharmacies and other essential services. And the cleaning staff who risked their lives to ensure safe

---

[2] See, for example, Williams, F. 2017. *The Nature Fix: Why Nature Makes Us Happier, Healthier, and More Creative.* New York: W.W. Norton & Company; and Louv, R. 2008. *Last Child in the Woods: Saving Our Children from Nature-Deficit Disorder.* Algonquin Books.

physical environments where people had to go to work in person, rather than sequestering at home.

Even more vital, the pandemic emphasized the important work of health care providers in all of their different roles—doctors, nurses, technicians, aides, custodians, administrators, and support staff who keep health care organizations running. And what about the work of caring for the vulnerable, community organizing, and ensuring that friends and neighbors are okay? How many of us really understood how valuable any of this work was prior to the pandemic? How many other occupations do we typically fail to value appropriately until they are at risk of evaporating entirely? I suspect that many people will have changed their minds about the value of all of this work as a consequence of this pandemic. But unless we change—transform—the practices, pay scales, and support for these types of work, there will be strong pressure to return, so far as possible, to business as usual so that current elites can maintain their power positions.

Possibly even more important is what Riane Eisler calls the caring economy[3]—work that is often done without the recognition of pay, but that proves vital during a crisis and is what holds societies together—it is where the value of relationship is most evident. Taking care of children, taking care of the ill or needy, taking care of the elderly. Volunteering in a whole array of arenas from food banks to child welfare to elderly support. Caring work builds on the values of relationship, reciprocity, redistribution, and responsibility for both self and other. Many people talk about the value of family—and friends. Similarly, with understanding local communities and neighborhoods—to which many people were introduced during the crisis, because they could go nowhere else.

Notably, it is the entire socio-political-economic system that needs to transform—not just the economic system, along with human beings' relationship with nature. As noted earlier, the neoliberal agenda ignored not only societal but also ecological impacts of economic activity. To get to

---

[3] Eisler, R. 2017. *The Real Wealth of Nations: Creating a Caring Economics*. San Francisco, CA: Berrett-Koehler Publishers; Eisler, R. 2017. "The Real Wealth of Nations: From Global Warming to Global Partnership." *Interdisciplinary Journal of Partnership 4*, no. 3 http://pubs.lib.umn.edu/ijps/vol4/iss3/13 (accessed May 27, 2020).

flourishing for all means including all humans and all other living beings on the planet. It also means including nature's ecosystems and the planet's ability to support flourishing life into the future.

A relational and life-affirming approach to transformation means shifting away from the dominance of markets to include recognition of the importance of all three of today's sectors—government, businesses, and civil society and what is sometimes called the fourth sector—"for benefit" hybrids that are evolving to combined market and social goals. Life, in other words, is not all about wealth maximization—at the individual level, company, or national level. It is about valuing what is really important, and finding ways for all people to belong and to use their voice to participate actively in the emergence of the world they actually want to live in. It means establishing workplaces where people can find meaning and purpose in their work, and use their voice—thus, shifting how enterprise, whether business or government, is organized so that such participation is possible. It means revaluing nature for her many gifts and stopping the exploitation that has nearly destroyed humanity's potential to survive.

As we each in our own ways think about how to move the system from today's dysfunctional patterns towards patterns that are more relational and life-centered to support flourishing for all, it is clear that our human production and natural systems, as well as human population growth, need to operate well within planetary boundaries. Difficult decisions need to be made to shift enterprises of all sorts away from their current paths, towards new ways of operating that incorporate principles that give life to the system. The disruption of the Covid-19 pandemic and ensuring crisis, however, has provided clear evidence that such shifts are entirely possible, given sufficient motivation. It has opened up many people's minds, including some policymakers, to the potential—and need—for such transformation.

Though this transformation may be difficult in the short term, particularly for organizations and people deeply embedded in today's ways of doing things, in the longer term it give hope. It is conceivable that everyone and every living organism will benefit from the shifts. That "every" includes people in all walks of life, businesses, and institutions of all sorts, from all nations both developed and still developing, and of all creeds and backgrounds. "Every" also includes nature's other living beings and the ecosystems that support them, since human flourishing intimately depends on flourishing natural systems in the world around us. Human beings, we know, are intricately connected to and part of nature and her ecosystems—not separate from or dominating over them. Every breath we take, every single thing we eat, all the resources we use come from nature. From the air we breathe to the materials from which we build our homes and businesses to the raw materials needed to cloth and feed us, never mind our pleasures, we depend on nature's bounty. When we begin to tell the new yet very ancient story that incorporates these ideas, we can each in our own way begin to move this transformation forward.

About the Author

Sandra Waddock is Galligan Chair of Strategy, Carroll School Scholar of Corporate Responsibility, and Professor of Management at Boston College's Carroll School of Management. Winner of numerous lifetime achievement awards, she has published 14 books and more than 150 papers and chapters in a wide variety of journals. Waddock's recent books include *Intellectual Shamans: Management and the Sustainability Paradox* (David Wasieleski, SW, and Paul Shrivastava, Taylor and Francis, in press), *Healing the World*, and *(Teaching) Managing Mindfully* (with Lawrence Lad and Judith Clair). Her 2008 book *The Difference Makers* won the Social Issues in Management Division (Academy of Management) best book and Intellectual Shamans won the best book for pedagogy from the International Humanistic Management Association. Current research interests are intellectual shamanism, transformational systems change, memes and narratives in system transformation, stewardship of the future, corporate sustainability and responsibility, the problem of growth, and wisdom. Waddock is a Councilor for the SDG Transformations Forum, a member of the Bounce Beyond Design Team, and the Global Assessment for New Economics, and an active participant in WEAll (Wellbeing Economy Alliance), the Academy of Management, and Humanistic Management networks, among other professional affiliations.

Index

Ackoff, R., 112
Alexander, C., 108
Alliance for Water Stewardship, 127
Anthropogenic (human-induced)
    warming, 24
Artificial intelligence (AI), 15
Autopoiesis, 110

B-Corporations, 161–162
Better Life Index, 96
Better Living Index, 96
Biocapacity, 29
Biodiversity loss, 27–28, 29
Blackmore, S., 61
Block, P., 124
Bocken, N.M., 151
Braungart, M., 108
Brundtland Commission Report, 54
Brundtland, G.H., 54
Business systems and employees
    cultural mythologies, 5–10
    future of jobs, 12–14
    hidden unemployment, 16–17
    inequality, 11–12
    offshoring and outsourcing, 15–16
    technologies, 15

Campbell, J., 55
Chaos theory, 85
Circular economy, 151–153
Circulatory system, 46
Civilizational collapse, 21
Collective value. *See also* Stewardship
    approach
    business, 118–120
    collective well-being, 120
    dignity violations, 121
    profitability and wealth
        maximization, 118–120
    purpose, 118
Collective well-being, 120
Conscious Capitalism, 163

Contextual interconnectedness, 109
Cooperatives, 165–166
Coral reefs, 29
Corporate social responsibility (CSR),
    114, 115
Covid-19, 20, 22, 31, 44, 169
Cradle-to-cradle design, 152
Crutzen, P.J., 27
Cultural mythologies, 5–10

Davis, G.F., 158, 159
Decarbonizing, 25
Deforestation, 28
Dehumanization, 17
Destructive externalities, 142
Diamond, J., 21, 85, 149
Dignity
    earth-and life-centric socio-
        economic perspective, 101
    Hicks arguement, 100
    nature's manifestations, 101
    practical perspective, 101
    Sen's arguement, 100
Diversity, 110–111
Donaldson, T., 118
Doughnut economics, 128
Dweck, C.S., 66
Dynamic interconnectedness, 48
Dysfunctional political and cultural
        practices
    annual trust survey, 31–32
    Covid-19 outbreak, 31
    failing infrastructure, 33
    Global Financial Crisis, 31
    inequality, 33
    obesity crisis, 32
    overconsumption patterns, 32

Earth stewardship, 124–125
Ecological/sustainability crises
    Anthropocene/era of human
        activity, 27

biodiversity loss, 27–28
  Great Acceleration, 26–27
  Intergovernmental Science-Policy
      Platform on Biodiversity, 30
  World Wildlife Organization,
      27–29
Economic system, 1–2
Economistic paradigm, 9
Economistic thinking, 9–10
Economists, 36–37
Edelman Trust Barometer, 31–32
Edge of chaos, 46, 48
Ehrenfeld, J., 54, 117, 148
Eisler, R., 177
Empiricism, 6
Employee stock ownership plan
      (ESOP), 166
Employment, 134
Enlightenment, 147
  beliefs, 5–6, 8
  economics, 8
  empiricism, 6
  Indigenous culture, 7
  quantitative approach, 8
  values, 7
  Western thinking, 6
Enlivenment, 147
Environmental, social, and
      governance (ESG)
      considerations, 143
Excellence through Stewardship
      initiative, 127
Externalities, 40–41, 141–142

Flourishing, 20
  indigenous culture, 104
      reciprocity, 106–107
      redistribution, 107
      relationship, 105, 107
      responsibility, 106
  indigenous wisdom, 103
  living systems, 108–111
  sustainability, 103
Forests, 29
Forest Stewardship Council, 126
Formal medium-sized enterprises, 160
Fossil fuels, 137
Foster long-termism, 144–145

Freeman, R.E., 119

Geissdoerfer, M., 151
Genuine Progress Indicator (GPI),
      98, 99
Gladwell, M., 85
Global Financial Crisis, 31
Global fisheries, 29
Global jobs crisis, 12–14
Global mindsets, 67
Global Reporting Initiative (GRI),
      143
Global warming, 22–25
Great Acceleration, 26–27
Greenhouse gases (GHGs) emissions,
      23
Gross domestic product (GDP), 98
Gross Happiness Indicator (GNH),
      98
Gross National Happiness Index, 98
Gross national product (GNP), 98
Growth-at-all-costs
      mentality, 10
      model, 153–154
Growth mindset, 67

Happiness, 93
Hardin, G., 124
Healthy complex systems, 48
Heinberg, R., 150
Helliwell, J.F., 93, 94
Hicks, D., 100
Hidden unemployment, 16–17
Hoffman, A., 54, 117, 148
Holons, 45–46

Iconic image, 61–62
Inclusive capitalism, 163
Indigenous culture, 7, 57
Indigenous peoples, 169
Individual freedom, 88
Industrialization, 35
Inequality, 11–12
Inequitable practices, 21
Integrated reporting (IR), 143–144
Intergovernmental Panel on Climate
      Change (IPCC), 22–25, 150

Intergovernmental Science-Policy
    Platform on Biodiversity
    (IPBES), 30
Internalized costs, 143
International Cooperative Alliance,
    165
International Integrated Reporting
    Council (IIRC), 143
International Labor Organization,
    134, 165

Jacobs, J., 111
James, W., 65
Job production, 134

Kennedy, B, 98
Klein, G., 67
Koestler, A., 45
Kramer, M.R., 145

Land Stewardship Project, 126
Life- and flourishing-centric narratives
    Genuine Progress Indicator, 99
    initiatives, 96
    quality of life dimensions, 97
    Sen and Nussbau's capabilities,
        95–97
    well-being, 93–94, 98
Life-giving perspectives and practices
    circularity, 151–153
    company localization, 156
    enough concept, 153–154
    financialization, 158
    mega-corporations, 157
    nongrowth-oriented economy,
        152–155
    resilience and diversity, 157–158
    right-sized communities, 155–156
    small firm, 159
    surveillance capitalism, 159
    systemic resilience, 155
    trade and business opportunities,
        156–157
Living Planet Index, 28
Living soil, 28
Living systems, 46
    contextual interconnectedness, 109
    novelty, 110

permeable containment, 109–110
requisite diversity, 110–111
socioeconomic systems, 108–109
wholeness, 111
Lovelock, J.E., 102

MacArthur Foundation, 152
Marine Stewardship Council, 127
McDonough, W., 108
McKinsey Global Institute, 15
Medium-sized enterprises (SME), 160
Mega-corporations, 157
Memeplexes, 62
Memes
    Apple logo, 62
    Coca-Cola symbol, 62
    iconic image, 61–62
    internet, 61
    language, 61
    memeplexes, 62
    and mindset, 64–67
    resonant, 62
    shared, 62
    words and phrases, 63
Mindset, 64–67
Monbiot, G., 37, 40, 55
Mont Pelerin Society, 36, 37

Nations, 46
Natural ecosystems, 50
Negative externalities, 142
Neoclassical economics, 4, 9
Neoliberal capitalism, 128
Neoliberal economic approach, 129
Neoliberalism, 2
    cultural mythology, 36
    dominant paradigm, 10
    economists, 36–37
    enlightenment era, 35
    externalities, 40–41
    human civilization, 36
    human population, 35
    industrial era, 35–36
    Monbiot's ideas, 37–38
    neoliberal policies, 40
    obesity crisis, 41
    Powell Memorandum, 38–39
    Reagan and Thatcher's election, 40

stories and narratives. *See* Stories
    and narratives
Neoliberal narrative, 87–88
Neoliberal thinking, 11
New economics, 68
"No alternative" belief, 68
Nongrowth-oriented economy,
    152–155
Nonpolluting energy, 137
Novelty, 110

Obesity crisis, 32
Ocean health, 29
Offshoring, 15–16
One-size-fits-all story, 60
Organisation for Economic Co-
    operation and Development
    (OECD), 96, 167
Outsourcing, 15–16
Overseas Development Institute
    (ODI), 16–17
Oxfam report, 11–12

Pelerin, M., 36, 37
PERMA model, 94–95
Permeable containment, 109–110
Piketty, T., 36
Planetary boundaries, 25–26
Planetary stewardship, 123
Planetary warming, 25
Pollution, 40
Porter, M.E., 145
Powell, L.F., 38
Predictability, 51
Produce quality products/services,
    138–139
Product stewardship, 127
Product Stewardship Institute, 127

Raworth's approach to economics,
    128
Raworth's doughnut model, 136
Reciprocity, 106–107
Redistribution, 107
Regenerative economy, 151–153
Relationship, 105
Relative decoupling, 149
Renewable energy, 137

Requisite diversity, 50, 110–111
Resonant memes, 62
Responsibility, 106
Rhinesmith, S.H., 67
Right-sized communities,
    155–156

Savaget, P., 151
Self-induced systemic crises
    climate change
        covid-19 infections, 22
        dehumanizing others, 21
        Diamond's civilizational collapse,
            21
        ecological/sustainability crises,
            26–30
        humanity, 21
        Intergovernmental Panel on
            Climate Change, 22–25
    Covid-19 pandemic, 20
    dysfunctional political and cultural
        practices, 30–33
    planetary boundaries, 25–26
Self-sufficiency model, 157
Seligman, M., 94
Servicizing, 140–141
Shared flourishing, 92
Sheth, J.N., 119
Sisodia, R., 119
Social enterprises, 163
Socially threatening, 169
Social media, 174
Societal changes, 148
Socioecological cliff, 34
Socio-economic systems, 46, 108–109
Software updates and improvements,
    141
Spengler, L., 153
Spikins, P., 104
State-owned enterprises (SOEs),
    167–168
Stewardship approach
    broad time and space scales, 124
    business associations, 127
    business purpose, 131
    business-related initiatives,
        126–127
    collective value

collaborate and compete,
135–137
communal benefit, 132
companies responsibility, 132
development, 133–134
employment and job production,
134
energy usage, 137
equitable decent wages and job
security, 135
externality, 141–142
Foster long-termism, 144–145
integrated reporting (IR),
143–144
internalized costs, 143
nature of innovation, 137–138
performance metrics, 131, 132
quality products/services,
138–140
servicizing, 140–141
software updates and
improvements, 141
universal basic income, 134–135
earth stewardship, 124–125
firm repurposing, 131
neoliberal capitalism, 128
neoliberal economic approach, 129
planetary stewardship, 123, 126
practices and policy changes,
130–131
Raworth's approach, 128
share-oriented corporation
ownership, 131
transformational change, 126
voluntary initiatives, 129
whole system, 127
Stockholm Resilience Centre, 25–26,
128
Stories and narratives
Campbell's story, 55–56
economic mindset, 67
exploitation, 54
externalities, 54
indigenous peoples, 60–61
initiatives, 68–69
Korten's assumption, 57
memes, 61–63
Monbiot's points, 55

neoliberal story, 58
neoliberal thinking, 54
"no alternative" belief, 68
one-size-fits-all story, 60
origin stories, 57
public and policy contexts, 59
sustainable development, 54
systemic change, 59
Vogler's view, 56
Subjective well-being, 93–94
Sufficiency economy, 153–154
Surveillance capitalism, 34, 159
Sustainability, 103
Sustainable development, 54
System change
dimensions, 85
gathering and reconciling, 86
institutions, 86
memes, 86
new narrative, 86
African cultures, 88
climate change issues, 90
common good, 89–90
economic and material growth,
89
flourishing, 91, 92
Freya Williams of Futerra, 87
Global Financial Crisis, 92
globalization, 88
individual freedom, 88, 91
memes, 90
neoliberal narrative, 87–88
recognition, 89
wealth maximization, 92
Systemic flourishing
companies, 115–116
corporate social responsibility
(CSR), 114, 115
Corporation2020 initiative, 117
corporations, 114
Delaware law, 113
ecological and systemic
sustainability, 117–118
humanity and systemic integrity, 116
institutional level, 118
institutions, 116–117
national level, 118
organizational level, 115

public institutions, 113
responsibility, 112
System transformation
change, 43
climate change and sustainability
crises, 43
complex adaptive systems, 43
covid-19 pandemic, 44
crisis, 44
economy, 43
living systems, 44
socioeconomic systems, 43
stakeholders, 42

Take-back approach, 141
"Take-make-waste" approach, 139
Thatcher, M., 68
Thunberg, G., 22
Topsoil and land degradation, 29–30
Tragedy of the commons, 124
Transformation
activity interest, 172
changing mindsets, 172
citizens and activist, 1745–179
Green New Deal, 170
networks, 173–174
paid work, 174
relational and life-affirming
approach, 170, 178
scope, 171
social media, 174
socio-political-economic system,
177–178
stories and narratives, 171–172
talent and skills, 173
work environment, 174
Transformative system change, 45

Ubuntu, 88, 106
United Nation's Human Development
Index (HDI), 98, 99
Universal basic income, 134–135

Vogler, C., 56

Walsh, J., 118
Wealth maximization, 92
Weber, A., 43
Well-being, 20, 93–94
collective, 96
gross domestic (national) product,
98
happiness, 93
subjective, 94
Well-being Economy Alliance
(WEAll), 3
Western thinking, 6
Whole living systems, 111
Whole systems, 46
Wickedness
and complexity, 47–49
problems, 46–47
and societies
depth in large systems, 50
healthy ecosystems, 49–50
predictability, 51
sectors, 49
stakeholders, 51
wicked problems, 50–51
socioecological systems, 47
transformative system
change, 51
Wolfe, D., 119
World Wildlife Organization (WWF)
report, 27–30

OTHER TITLES IN THE BUSINESS ETHICS AND CORPORATE CITIZENSHIP COLLECTION

David Wasieleski, Duquesne University, Editor

- *Applied Humanism* by Jennifer Hancock
- *Powerful Performance* by Mark Eyre

Concise and Applied Business Books

The Collection listed above is one of 30 business subject collections that Business Expert Press has grown to make BEP a premiere publisher of print and digital books. Our concise and applied books are for...

- Professionals and Practitioners
- Faculty who adopt our books for courses
- Librarians who know that BEP's Digital Libraries are a unique way to offer students ebooks to download, not restricted with any digital rights management
- Executive Training Course Leaders
- Business Seminar Organizers

Business Expert Press books are for anyone who needs to dig deeper on business ideas, goals, and solutions to everyday problems. Whether one print book, one ebook, or buying a digital library of 110 ebooks, we remain the affordable and smart way to be business smart. For more information, please visit www.businessexpertpress.com, or contact sales@businessexpertpress.com.

www.ingramcontent.com/pod-product-compliance
Lightning Source LLC
Chambersburg PA
CBHW052108230326
41599CB00054B/4701